W9-BHM-708

Pluralism in Management

Routledge Studies in Management, Organisation and Society

This series presents innovative work grounded in new realities, addressing issues crucial to an understanding of the contemporary world. This is the world of organised societies, where boundaries between formal and informal, public and private, local and global organizations have been displaced or have vanished, along with other nineteenth century dichotomies and oppositions. Management, apart from becoming a specialized profession for a growing number of people, is an everyday activity for most members of modern societies.

Similarly, at the level of enquiry, culture and technology, and literature and economics, can no longer be conceived as isolated intellectual fields; conventional canons and established mainstreams are contested. Management, Organization and Society addresses these contemporary dynamics of transformation in a manner that transcends disciplinary boundaries, with books that will appeal to researchers, student and practitioners alike.

12. Pluralism in Management
Organizational Theory, Management
Education, and Ernst Cassirer
Eirik J. Irgens

Management Theory
A critical and reflexive reading
Nanette Monin

Other titles in this series:

Contrasting Involvements
A study of management accounting
practices in Britain and Germany
Thomas Ahrens

Turning Words, Spinning Worlds
Chapters in Organizational Ethnography
Michael Rosen

Breaking Through the Glass Ceiling
Women, power and leadership in
agricultural organizations
Margaret Alston

The Poetic Logic of Administration
Styles and changes of style in the art
of organizing
Kaj Sköldberg

Casting the Other
Maintaining gender inequalities
in the workplace
Edited by Barbara Czarniawska and
Heather Höpfl

**Gender, Identity and the Culture of
Organizations**
Edited by Iiris Aaltio and
Albert J. Mills

Text/Work
Representing organization and
organizing representation
Edited by Stephen Linstead

**The Social Construction of
Management**
Texts and identities
Nancy Harding

'In this book Irgens offers a fresh take on organizational understanding by being among the first writers to transpose Cassirer's thinking to organization studies. The idea of consistently exploring organizational richness while not losing sight of the organizational surface is challenging and promising for management education as well as for consulting. The book adds to our understanding of organization as process.'

Tor Hernes, Copenhagen Business School, Denmark

Pluralism in Management

Organizational Theory,
Management Education, and Ernst Cassirer

Eirik J. Irgens

Routledge
Taylor & Francis Group
New York   London

EDUC

HM
786
.I74
2011

First published 2011
by Routledge
711 Third Avenue, New York, NY 10017

Simultaneously published in the UK
by Routledge
2 Park Square, Milton Park, Abingdon, Oxon OX14 4RN

Routledge is an imprint of the Taylor & Francis Group, an informa business

© 2011 Taylor & Francis

The right of Eirik J. Irgens to be identified as author of this work has been asserted by him in accordance with sections 77 and 78 of the Copyright, Designs and Patents Act 1988.

Typeset in Sabon by IBT Global.
Printed and bound in the United States of America on acid-free paper by IBT Global.

Library of Congress Cataloging-in-Publication Data
Irgens, Eirik J., 1955–
   Pluralism in management : organizational theory, management education, and Ernst Cassirer / Eirik J. Irgens.
      p. cm. — (Routledge studies in management, organizations, and society ; 12)
   Includes bibliographical references and index.
   ISBN 978-0-415-88617-8
   1. Cassirer, Ernst, 1874–1945.   2. Organizational sociology—Philosophy.
   3. Pluralism.   I. Title.
   HM786.I74 2011
   302.3'5—dc22
   2010045868

ISBN13: 978-0-415-88617-8 (hbk)
ISBN13: 978-0-203-81708-7 (ebk)

Contents

Tables

Figures

Abbreviations

Introduction

My motivation for writing about Cassirer is not based on a wish to investigate philosophy, as such. Consequently, where philosophers expect to find lengthy discussions about, for example, the different branches of the Marburg school, they will be disappointed. I am not investigating Cassirer in order to shed light on philosophy. Also, taking into account the diversity and enormous number of subjects covered by Cassirer in his writings, I will leave several themes unnoticed.

It is thus important to emphasize that my point of departure is as an organizational theorist with a background in the practice of organizational development; learning and change; and a particular interest for how we, including myself, may become better practitioners in our organizational work, whether we are theorizing or practicing organization in academia or in what is often referred to as "real life" and "real organizations." How can we understand organizations in ways that are useful to us? How can we obtain a realistic view of the processes of organizing and the forms we call organizations (and, sometimes, institutions)? How can we train ourselves to become better organizational theorists and practitioners, based on close, practice-based, and realistic understandings of organizational life? How can we educate managers and professionals to become experts in their fields?

Developing an understanding of organizations based on Cassirer's philosophy is a long shot. My attempt is merely a modest effort to open some doors that may or may not lead to a new understanding. It is driven by my own curiosity about these philosophical ideas that, if a counterfactual history of the philosophical underpinnings of organizational theory were written, most likely would have led to a different landscape of organization theory than we see around us today.

I am grateful to Turid, who not only led me to Ernst Cassirer but also through her paintings and drawings introduced me to the power of the fine arts, as well as to the mystery that is to be found if one bothers to look beneath formal surfaces. I also wish to express my gratitude to Daved Barry and Stefan Meisiek and to my colleagues at Nord Trondelag

University College (HiNT) and Learning Lab Denmark—in particular, Hans Siggaard Jensen, who believed in me. I am also grateful to the amazing Henrik Nitschke, who makes servant leadership something more than a buzzword.

1 An Autobiographical Account of a Formative Experience

I suppose we all have had some formative experiences that have shaped us as persons or, if one can make such a distinction, as professionals.

I certainly have had such experiences. Being locked in a hotel for five days with sixty other scared managers and some consultants and psychiatrists trained in unstructured processes in the Tavistock tradition definitely did something to me, although I cannot explain exactly what. Being evaluated by my colleagues and subordinates using personality tests also had some effect. And sitting in a room with many other people and being told that some of us would be laid off, and then suddenly realizing how angst smells, is something that has followed me since.

Some episodes from my second career as an academic scholar have had a lasting impact, too. I will never forget some lectures where I am sure Csikszentmihalyi would have nodded his head and said that we all, both students and I, were in a flow, an autotelic situation where we became one and we all knew that what we were experiencing at that very moment was something very special. (I guess it is that feeling I always strive to recreate when I start my lectures, but is it difficult!) And I remember some episodes with colleagues when what I thought was an innocent discussion about different schools of management theory nearly ended in murder. (Who said that theory is detached from "real life"?)

But one experience stands out as particularly decisive for my current piece of writing. It goes back to the early 1990s.

TAKING TEXTBOOK KNOWLEDGE TO THE REAL WORLD

I was so proud. Top management had asked me to be in charge of the strategy process at Aker Verdal. Formally, the CEO would be in charge, of course; but I was the one who was going to design and lead the whole process. They had noticed my work in the Human Resource Department, and they trusted me, they said. This was my big chance.

I had worked at Aker Verdal, the offshore construction yard, a little more than two years. When I got the job, I had just finished my master's degree program at UC Davis. I knew what I was doing. I was a distinguished scholar at UCD. I had excellent grades. In other words, I was prepared for the task. But Aker Verdal surprised me. It was not like the companies in the textbooks. Everything seemed to change all the time. My first shock came after just a few weeks when the company lost a major contract. Suddenly, people all around me were laid off. There was no work for me, either. I had to work for a small company in a rural village. But after a few months, Aker Verdal won a new contract, and I was back in the yard again. This time the situation was different: there were not enough workers. We had to get welders from Denmark and from other parts of Norway. This should have been avoided, I thought; I was sure that they knew nothing about planning. Now I was expecting a more stable work situation, but the longed-for stability never came. Instead, I learned the meaning of hyper-turbulence: we planned for something only to realize that our assumptions were wrong when we arrived at work the following day. We lost contracts we had expected to win, and we won some that we never thought we would be even close to getting. And as soon as we started a new job, the customer (typically an oil company) changed the design, and then changed it again. The situation was disturbing.

Aker Verdal was and still is an offshore construction yard. The key products have been the engineering and building of large steel constructions (platforms, modules, and jackets), hulls, and wellhead platforms. The products are highly specialized. In addition, the scope constantly changes during a project period. In the late 1970s and early 1980s, about 20 Norwegian construction yards were competing with Aker Verdal. By 2003 only six were left, and Aker Verdal was the only one still building steel jackets. And at the same time, the global competition, also from the Far East, had become stronger every year, forcing Aker Verdal to compete with companies from economies with substantially lower personnel costs.

RATIONAL AND CREATIVE STRATEGY WORK

Although uncertainty and unpredictability characterized Aker Verdal, formal planning had always been central. Aker Verdal was jam-packed with elaborate planning systems. Strategy had traditionally been a long-range planning process based on external and internal analysis, resulting in formal plans. Aker Verdal was part of an international corporation with headquarters in Oslo, Norway. Each December–January the planning staff in Oslo analyzed markets and international trends. Their background document was the central guidance for the strategy process in each of the companies in the corporation. The idea was that the companies should position themselves in such a way as to make a complementary group of businesses. Such was the case in February of 1991, when the CEO called on me to help with the new strategy process. My task was to help top management develop a plan for the following two years. In cooperation with the CEO, I set up a time schedule for the process. By June, we were supposed to finish an overall plan for the whole company. On the basis of this plan, the different divisions were expected to develop their operational plans by November. The division plans were again starting points for more detailed plans that could be broken down into individual work plans.

The top management group was committed to the process. They agreed that each of them should carry out strategy analysis within their specific responsibility areas. These analyses would be used as chapters in the new strategy plan. Every second week of the month throughout spring, they met to do strategy work. I conducted these sessions. The CFO analyzed the financial situation and presented it to the others. The managers in charge of fabrication, human resources, technology, and market did parallel work within their responsibility areas. When it was the market manager's turn, he predicted that only the very best construction yards in Europe would survive the coming years because of low activity in the offshore market.

In addition to the biweekly top management meetings, two seminars were conducted in which middle management, labor representatives, and top management participated. The CEO and I led these sessions. The top management groups' analyses were presented, with an emphasis on the challenges of the new market situation. Then we worked in groups on how to meet the new challenges. This work was of two kinds: *rational* strategy work, which involved traditional analysis based on the planning and design school toolkits (e.g., gap analysis and SWOT); and *creative* work, with participants using colored pencils and giant sheets of paper to express their mental images of the company as they saw it at that time and as they expected it to be in three years.

My inspiration for the creative sessions came from Marjorie Parker (1990), who worked as a consultant in the Norwegian corporation Norsk Hydro's aluminum plant in Karmøy, Norway, in 1986. Hydro Aluminum was by then Europe's largest producer of aluminum; with 1,700 employees, the Karmøy plant (KF) was the largest of Hydro Aluminum's plants. In cooperation with KF's CEO, Parker conducted a visioning process that combined the Scandinavian democratic tradition with creative art-based methods. The Scandinavian way of conducting business is characterized by equality and consensus (Schramm-Nielsen et al. 2004). Marjorie Parker combined the willingness and expectation to participate in the decision-making processes that were part of the work culture with creative vision processes, which were less common in Norwegian companies. The CEO had previously engaged an artist to develop a visionary picture of the company's desired future, but was not satisfied with the result. Now Parker engaged the employees in a series of sessions in which they used crayons to develop colorful pictures of the company as a garden. Their vision led to action plans and, according to Parker, increased empowerment, focus, and commitment.

So the CEO and I had engineers, union representatives, and managers working in groups and expressing on large sheets of paper their artistic images of Aker Verdal in the past, in the present, and in the future. Some were reluctant, some cynical; but after a while, they all were busy discussing and drawing with colorful crayons.

When they were finished, the drawings decorated the walls. It would be a slight exaggeration to say that the results were impressive, at least assessed as works of art. But creating and discussing them was surely different from what they were used to doing. The groups took turns presenting their work. One group had pictured a person pumping iron, some new buildings, a piggy bank, and a person crossing the finishing line as number one. They explained the need to develop a focused strategic plan, invest in new assembly halls, improve logistics, and develop competence; in turn, it would become possible not only to compete with the best European plants, but to beat them all.

A second group portrayed Aker Verdal at the top of a winners' roster that said "European Champion 1997." In second place was Kvaerner, the fierce Norwegian competitor; in third place was the Italian plant Belleli. The group argued that if strategy work was taken seriously and if we worked hard on continuous improvement, Aker Verdal had a fair chance of becoming the number one plant in Europe.

After all the groups had presented their works of art, we had a lengthy plenary discussion. Out of the discussion came a vision: Aker Verdal was to become the best offshore construction yard in Europe within prioritized areas (e.g., steel jackets). I am not sure who initially formulated this idea; in retrospect, I remember it as something that "just emerged" from the groups' artwork and discussions.

The overall strategy plan was finished by June. The CEO, supported by the other top managers, conducted a series of meetings to communicate the new strategy to everyone. In these meetings, he presented the new strategy and legitimated it with the help of the SWOT and the market analysis from the overall strategy plan. The plan had become an immense document, crammed with numbers and impressive analysis. In August, the middle managers were to develop plans for their divisions and to align activities with the new strategy plan. The message now was *plan discipline*: "the plans were in charge," as we used to say; improvisation and local expensive solutions were banned.

THE SINKING OF THE SLEIPNER A PLATFORM

By August we were on schedule with the strategy work. The main task then was to fine-tune the rest of the company. Top management seemed to appreciate the way I had helped them with the process, and I was extremely proud of myself and the beautiful strategy plan.

On 23 August, I woke up to disturbing news. The Sleipner A platform had been sinking during testing in the Gandsfjord, close to Stavanger, Norway. The foundation leaked and sank during a controlled filling of ballast in connection with the assembly of the top site. When the 250,000-ton concrete platform hit the bottom of the fjord, it left nothing but a pile of debris 220 m deep and a seismic response reading of 3.0 on the Richter scale. Also the institutional field of oil and gas trembled: The cost was $700 million; but, even worse, the accident put at risk the largest Norwegian business contract everbecause the Sleipner A platform was built to supply Europe with gas through the Zeepipe pipeline to Zeebrugge in Belgium. To build a new concrete platform would take three years, a delay that would jeopardize the extremely important multibillion-dollar export contract. Thus, the Norwegian state oil company Statoil, today one of the world's largest exporters of crude oil, was looking for an alternative to building a new concrete platform. In the new strategy plan, we had positioned ourselves as experts on steel jackets. Statoil decided to ask Aker Verdal for help. A steel riser platform jacket would be faster to build, but would nevertheless normally take about a year to finish. To build it faster would require a total commitment to the project, including the dedication of human and other organizational resources, as well as flexibility and simplicity in the planning and construction process.

The sinking of the Sleipner A platform was never predicted in the strategy process or in the extensive plan that came out it. If Aker Verdal was to build the steel riser platform, the strategy plan seemed to be of little or no value. I was disappointed: my efforts seemed to be a waste of time.

FROM FORMAL PLANS TO PLANNING AND IMPROVISATION: A PERIOD OF IDEOLOGICAL EXCEPTION

No serious discussions took place. Top management accepted the challenge and put the strategy plan aside. Aker Verdal built the 4,330-ton Sleipner Riser platform and 1,900 tons of piles in about half the normal time. The exceptionally short building time was seen as close to impossible in the institutional field of oil and gas. In order to succeed, Aker Verdal abandoned established organizational practices. For example, there was no time for formal planning as the company knew it. During the building of the Sleipner Riser, planning and building often happened in parallel, and formal plans were sometimes developed more as documentation than as tools for work performance. The traditional way of organizing work was also put aside as long as the project lasted. The boundaries between Aker Verdal, Statoil, and subcontractors became blurred; and the pyramidal multilayer organization relying on mechanistic principles was, to a large degree, replaced by informal networks and self-organizing work groups.

The accident challenged the taken-for-granted assumptions underlying the dominating traditions of planning and organizing in the company. Planning and the use of sophisticated planning tools had always been fundamental at Aker Verdal. When Aker Verdal accepted the Sleipner Riser contract, "the traditional way of doing things" was put aside, but only for the project period. Work was based less on formal plans and more on continuous planning and improvisation. This change was a success. But the abandonment of the well-established ways of planning and working was seen as an ideological exception. When Sleipner Riser was successfully delivered to Statoil, it was back to business as usual.

THE CHAMELEON'S EYES

I have illustrated how the strategy process was designed and performed on the micro level: how it was led, who participated, and what activities were performed, as well as how a major discontinuity suddenly changed the rules of the game. It was tempting to conclude "Learning 1, Planning 0," as Henry Mintzberg (1991) did in his classical strategy dispute with "the Father of Strategic Management," Igor Ansoff (1991). However, I came to understand that such dualism would be oversimplicity, a closure that actually could hinder learning. On the one hand, I admitted that "my" strategy plan and all the meticulous rational analysis seemed to have little value as operational and predictive support alone because the premises changed so abruptly. On the other hand, they also seemed to play an imperative role in combination with the art-based processes; I was just not sure how.

It appeared that the new company vision—a result of both rational analysis and creative sessions—seemed to fuel a collective mindset and a stronger organizational commitment. A survey among 15,000 employees in different Nordic companies revealed that in no other company did employees have a stronger belief in the future of their own organization than those at Aker Verdal. It was difficult to distinguish which of the processes was most important. The creative work in the strategy process grew out of a new understanding that was the result of rational analysis; and the creative work seemed to open perspectives, add flavor, and attach meaning to the piles of numbers in the strategy analysis. I concluded that both ways of working had been important.

When Claus Nygaard invited me to lecture before the strategy students at Copenhagen Business School, I used the Aker Verdal strategy case to advocate the view that the design/planning and pattern/learning schools should not be seen as mutually exclusive dichotomies, but as representing different processes whereby one constitutes the other in an interdependent yin/yang manner, and that organizational deep-level and surface-level elements should be seen as parts of the same processes. However, when only one gains ideological dominance, the ability to solve real problems in a complex and changing context is reduced, I claimed. At Aker Verdal, an organizational ideology based on such values as clear norms and rules, top-down management, disciplinary control, detailed planning, a high degree of formalization, and hierarchical organization had developed into a taken-for-granted metastandard for organizing. Improvisation and planning as a continuous process had become illegitimate activities that were allowed during only the limited period when the Riser Platform was built. When the Sleipner Riser was finished, the old order was reestablished.

This strategy case turned out to be a formative experience to me. When we think about formative experiences, we often think of incidents that have shaped our character and formed us in important ways. I was not "formed" in the sense that I found the answers; I rather found some new questions. A certain curiosity and some questions were formed that guided me for years to come. It was a new awareness, not in the form of some religious or spiritual revelation, but an inquisitiveness that turned my focus from either-or to a more relational and combined view: surface *and* deep-level phenomena, facts *and* values, knowledge as a thing *and* as a process, science *and* art, rationality *and* emotions, functionalistic *and* interpretive. It was like trying to imitate the chameleon's eyes. The funny thing about the chameleon, in addition to its well-known ability to change colors according to the landscape, is its ability to focus its eyes on different objects at the same time, and still obtain an accurate view, as well as a better overview, of the whole situation. It started as a hunch, a suspicion that developing the ability to "see" would turn me into a better organizational developer and change agent. When I reentered the academic world, this combined focus guided my scholarship—my reading, writing, and teaching—and inspired me to produce this work.

Turning the page to the next chapter, some readers might find it strange to start reading about Ernst Cassirer's philosophy and debates within the philosophical community in the 1920s. But I hope the reader will stay tuned. Something there actually still has consequences for how we think about and carry out theory and practice today.

2 Cassirer's Philosophy of Symbolic Forms

This chapter introduces Cassirer's philosophy of symbolic forms. I discuss briefly how Cassirer drew on Hegel as well as on Kant, how he differed from these thinkers, and how the idea of the symbolic forms was developed into a plural and non-dualistic[1] theory of knowledge. I close the chapter by summarizing why I find Cassirer particularly relevant to organizational theory and management education.

UNVEILING THE ULTIMATE REALITY

After concentrated studies at the Warburg Library in 1922–1925, Ernst Cassirer (1874–1945) released his three volumes of *The Philosophy of Symbolic Forms: Language* (*PSF* 1) in 1923, *Mythical Thought* (*PSF* 2) in 1925, and *The Phenomenology of Knowledge* (*PSF* 3) in 1929. Cassirer analyzed how three major areas of man's cultural life—myth, language, and science—were structured logically, and showed how space, time, cause, substance, and number as general categories of thought obtained content differently within these three symbolic forms (Verene 1969: 40–41).

The symbolic forms are areas of man's cultural life, illustrating the historical development of human consciousness, and representing different logics and angles of refraction that man can take on to understand reality. They are not to be understood as classes of perceptions or objects; rather, they represent different perspectives that can be taken of any object, according to Verene. In *The Philosophy of Symbolic Forms*, Cassirer chose to discuss myth, language, and science as focal symbolic forms. However, fifteen years later, in *An Essay on Man* (1944; from now on abbreviated *EoM*) he included chapters on religion, history, and art as well. In *Mythical Thought*, he also mentioned the possibility that ethics, law, economics, and technology could be treated as symbolic forms (*PSF* 2: xiv–xv).

Donald Phillip Verene (1969) concluded:
It seems clear that for Cassirer any area of culture is potentially a symbolic form; and whether any area of culture is a symbolic

form would appear determined by whether it can be shown to have a distinctive logical structure. For Cassirer, in a manner analogous to Hegel, all symbolic forms are potentially present in each stage of consciousness.

(Verene 1969: 44)

According to Cassirer, reality is cloaked as well as revealed in the symbolic forms (*PSF* 3: 1). Symbolic forms open, illuminate, and hide reality. They offer different perspectives, angles, and logics that may shed light on, or veil, aspects of reality. Cassirer sees his philosophy as an endeavor into the distinctiveness of these different forms. "The same basic functions which give the world of the spirit its determinacy, its imprint, its character, appear on the other side to be so many refractions which an intrinsically unitary and unique being undergoes as soon as it is perceived and assimilated by a "subject." Seen from this standpoint," Cassirer holds forth;

" . . . the philosophy of symbolic forms is nothing other than an attempt to assign each of them, as it were, its own specific and peculiar index of refraction. The philosophy of symbolic forms aspires to know the special nature of the various refracting media, to understand each one according to its nature and the laws of its structure.

(*PSF* 3: 1)

Cassirer explained his philosophical journey as an attempt to unveil the ultimate reality, the reality of "being" itself. He quoted Spinoza as saying that it is the essence of light to illumine itself and the darkness, so at some point there must be an immediate self-revelation and reality. Epistemologically, he claims that ". . . thought and reality ought not merely to correspond to each other in some sense but must permeate each other" (*PSF* 3: 2). The function of thought should not be merely to "express" being, or to apprehend and classify it under one of its own categories of meaning. Thought should instead "deal with reality on equal footing" (*PSF* 3: 2). Thought and the object toward which it is directed are one, and are not to be treated as separated unities. As I hope to show in this book, this non-dualistic and relational stance permeates Cassirer's philosophy and is among the central characteristics of his position between the analytic and the radical philosophical schools.

CASSIRER'S MAIN POINTS OF DEPARTURE

Verene (1969) pointed out that most commentators understand Cassirer's philosophy of symbolic forms as basically derived from Kant. However, Verene claimed that Cassirer built the presuppositions of "symbolic forms" on Hegel, rather than on Kant. He referred to Cassirer himself, who regarded Hegel's *Phenomenology of Mind* (which appeared in 1807) as the foundation work of his own *The Philosophy of Symbolic Forms*: "In defending his theory of symbolic forms and the theory of man that underlies it Cassirer selects Hegel rather than Kant," Verene (1969) concluded, and held forth that the problems Cassirer's commentators raise concerning Cassirer's philosophy can be largely solved through attention to Cassirer's relationship with Hegel (36). Lofts (2000), writing from a viewpoint as a continental philosopher, and more specifically from a viewpoint as a structuralist, interpreted the philosophy of symbolic forms as " . . . a *type* of 'structuralism' *avant la lettre* resulting from a fusion and critical transformation of Kant's critical transcendental philosophy, on the one hand, and Hegel's phenomenology of spirit, on the other" (21). Lofts stated that Cassirer's philosophy is "neither neo-Kantian nor neo-Hegelian," but a synthesis of number of thinkers: Heraclitus, Kant, Hegel, Natorp, Goethe, Schelling, Husserl; " . . . to mention a few" (21–22).

In agreement with Verene as well as Lofts, Neher (2005) pointed out that Cassirer's philosophy of symbolic forms is derived from both Kant and Hegel. But Neher nevertheless underscored the significant role of Kant in Cassirer's thinking: "Kant was the philosopher who most effectively broke the hold of the idea that our knowledge of the empirical world is simply a case of consciousness mirroring a preestablished reality that exists independently of our apprehension of it" (359). Also, Cassirer undoubtedly belonged to the neo-Kantian Marburg school, of which Hermann Cohen (1842–1918) and Paul Natorp (1854–1924) were among the most central philosophers. The Marburg school built on and reinterpreted Kant in an effort to develop a non-dualistic philosophy.

In contrast with the Marburg school, we find the rivaling neo-Kantian Baden school (also known as the Heidelberger school and the Southwest school). Among its significant members were Wilhelm Windelband (1848–1915), Emil Lask (1875–1915), Heinrich Rickert (1863–1936), and Max Weber (1864–1920).

These two schools interpreted Kant differently. The Baden school placed more emphasis on science and logics, and built on a dualist notion of subject and object, knowledge and reality, concept and object, form and subject matter. The world out there is infinite, and no way or method exists that may help us experience the world "as it is" (Birkeland 1993; Birkeland and Nilsen 2002). In contrast, the Marburg school held that subject and object do not belong to separate worlds; rather, they are in a relational process with each other. Experience and consciousness are not abstract entities; and reality is something that is ontologically finite and can, although never fully, be grasped through experience. To the Baden school, the world is, so to speak, "out of reach." Thus, the Baden school rejected positivism and reinforced the divide between natural and interpretive sciences.[2]

"Cassirer worked all his life to develop a systematic philosophy able to overcome the dualism of the Baden school," according to Foss and Kasa (2002: 14). In doing so, he seems to have reinterpreted the Marburg school's neo-Kantian stance by drawing on Hegel's dialectical and historical theory of the development of human knowledge. Cassirer's philosophy is a philosophy of man, a cultural philosophy where the development of man's consciousness throughout history is pivotal. Every stage of consciousness represents certain symbolic forms. In different stages, different forms are more dominating than in others, and influence the way man understands his own particular being. As a crude simplification, one may say that man's consciousness has developed from a mythical to a scientific stage. Other forms of knowing exist in parallel at a certain historical stage, but the logics and levels of refraction that the particular form of science represents have become increasingly dominant.

According to Verene (1969: 39), Cassirer regarded Hegel's distinction between science and sensory consciousness as analogous to his own distinction between science and mythical knowledge. Hegel analyzed the progress of man's consciousness as a development from an immediate sensory-based understanding to an advanced level of scientific understanding, as I have tried to depict in Figure 2.1.

Cassirer built on Hegel's idea, but developed it into a theory of culture and *various forms of knowledge*. "Cassirer (. . .) regards mythical consciousness as an earlier and more fundamental stage of mind than Hegel's stage of sensory consciousness," Verene held forth (1969: 35–36). By using the term "mythical" instead of "sensory," Cassirer avoided giving the impression that understanding can be a totally pure sensory consciousness, unmolded by the forms of knowing that are represented by a certain stage of man's cultural development. What characterizes man is that human knowledge is *symbolic*.

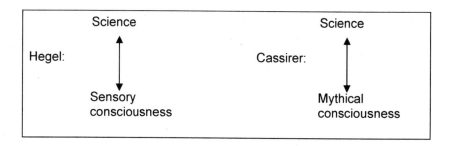

Figure 2.1 Sensory versus mythical consciousness in Hegel's and Cassirer's philosophies.

SYMBOLIC FORMS AS STAGES IN THE DEVELOPMENT OF MAN

In The Phenomenology of Knowledge, Cassirer—like Hegel in the Phenomenology of Mind—distinguished three major stages in the historical development of the mind. Like Hegel, he described these stages in terms of the mind's relationship to its objects. However, their philosophies were different in some ways. Hegel's phenomenology addresses a development from Bewusstsein (conscious) to Selbstbewusstsein (self-conscious) leading to an Aufheben to Geist/mind, as illustrated in Figure 2.2.

"The first of Cassirer's functions is the expressive function of consciousness (*Ausdrucksfunktion*), the second is the representational function (*Darstellungsfunktion*), and the third is the conceptual function (*reine Bedeutungsfunktion*)," following Verene (1969: 38) who depicted these three functions as standing in a dialectical relationship to each other. The expressive function represents a stage where there is a "simple unity of symbol and object." Symbol and object is one, there is no genuine distinction (symbol=object). The representational function is a stage where symbol and object are separated and viewed as totally different from each other (symbol≠object). At the conceptual stage this severance is overcome: Now the object is seen as a construction of the symbol. As such it becomes a symbol as well, but it is viewed as a symbol of different order (symbol–object).

Verene pointed out that there is a correspondence between Cassirer's three stages and the three stages of Hegel's phenomenology. Their progression parallels Hegel's conception of aufheben " (. . .) in which each stage

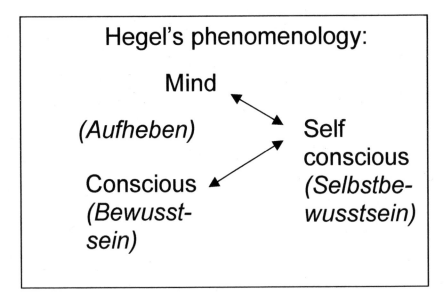

Figure 2.2   The dialectics of Hegel's phenomenology of the mind.

is both the cancellation and the preservation of the stage before it" (Verene 1969: 38). I have illustrated Cassirer's dialectics in Figure 2.3.

Summing up his discussion of the philosophical roots of Cassirer's philosophy of symbolic form, Verene states:

> Cassirer's phenomenology differs from Hegel's in three major respects: (1) its conception of the fundamental stage of consciousness and the consequent alignment of succeeding stages; (2) its method of description of each stage; and (3) its lack of a terminating stage of philosophical knowledge.
>
> (Verene 1969: 39)

In the following section, I will inquire into the idea of symbolic forms, with a special eye for the particularities that I find most relevant to the study of organizations and the teaching of management.

REALITY CLOAKED AND REVEALED IN SYMBOLIC FORMS

Discussing the methodological beginning of natural science, Cassirer pointed to a *regressus ad infinitum,* or everlasting regression. Behind all reality held to be true and objective, another reality will arise. It is impossible to call a halt to this progress and so secure an absolute solid "foundation" of knowledge (*PSF* 3: 19). According to Cassirer, even the modern physicist tends to dismiss any epistemological doubt as to the definitive

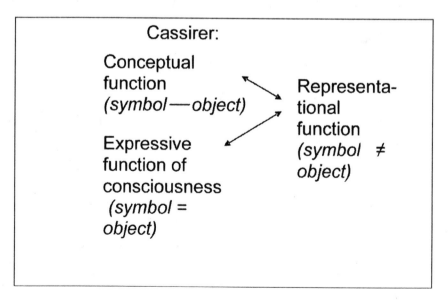

Figure 2.3 Cassirer's three major stages in the historical development of the mind.

character of his concept of reality. With the German physicist Max Planck (1858–1947), considered the founder of quantum theory, Cassirer found what he saw as a conclusive definition of reality in the identification of the real with the measurable. Cassirer found this realm of the measurable to sustain itself and to be self-explanatory. Natural sciences shun the method of dialectic thinking due to anxiety about being undermined (*PSF* 3: 19). Cassirer stated, "The positivists are incapable of expressing and exhausting the truly positive aspects of psychology through their positive theory of knowledge" (*PSF* 3: 27).

To Cassirer, the world is given to us through immediate sensations. It breaks down into a diversity of sensory impressions. However, classification does not necessarily lead to concreteness and determinacy, as illustrated by Cassirer in his classification of primitive sense perceptions (e.g., smells and colors). The role of language is to designate determinate qualities, but these processes usually proceed indirectly; an abstraction of smell is, for example, not possible. The designation of determinate qualities proceeds indirectly through substances that it has coined on the basis of other sensory-intuitive data (*PSF* 3: 129).

The senses are qualitatively different. In the highest objective senses (hearing and vision), a distance is achieved, according to Cassirer. A trend towards representation is unmistakably present and unfulfilled, in the sense that the "objective" content stops "at the limit of our own body." The tactile sense is somehow different, however, in the way that it represents an important step toward raising impressions to representations. The tactile sense has been called the true sense of reality—a sense whose phenomena have the most efficient sense of reality. But even though the tactile sense has a peculiar tendency toward objectivization, it stops halfway. It remains bipolar in the sense that we have a subjective component, relating to our body, which inevitably goes hand in hand with another component, oriented toward things and their attributes (*PSF* 3: 130). Reality and representative function are one, Cassirer concluded as he made his non-dualistic stance clear: "For the reality of a phenomenon cannot be separated from its representative function; it ceases to be the same as soon as it signifies something different, as soon as it points to another total complex as its background" (*PSF* 3: 141).

THE PROBLEM OF THE REPRESENTATION

In *Language,* Cassirer dwelled on the problem of representation. The whole is not obtained from its parts; on the contrary, every notion of a part already encompasses the notion of the whole, as to general structure and form, not as to content. Every particular belongs to a definite complex: "It is the totality of these rules which constitutes the true unity of consciousness, as a unity of time, space, objective synthesis, etc." (*PSF* 1: 102). He asserted that the traditional language of psychology does not offer an entirely adequate term for these states of affairs, with one exception: only through Gestalt psychology has the discipline moved away from what Cassirer considered fundamental sensationalism. "For the sensationalist approach, which sees all objectivity as encompassed in the 'simple' impression, synthesis consists merely in the 'association' of impressions" (*PSF* 1: 102). "Association" may have many meanings, but Cassirer did not believe that the sensationalist approach shed light on " . . . the diversity of the paths and directions by which consciousness arrives at its synthesis" (*PSF* 1: 103).

Here we see Cassirer preparing the groundwork for the theory of symbolic forms. Human consciousness is formed by historically developed forms of knowledge. It is inevitably molded by symbolic forms, and understanding cannot be a totally pure sensory consciousness, unmolded by the forms of knowing that are represented by a certain stage of man's cultural development. Human knowledge is symbolic knowledge.

Cassirer believed that in the true synthesis of consciousness, the relationship between the parts is fundamentally surpassed by the relationship of the "whole" to the "parts." "Here the whole does not *originate* in its parts, it *constitutes* them and gives them their essential meaning" (*PSF* 1: 103). We relate a limited segment of space to the whole of space: thinking of a particular moment of time, we encompass the universal form of succession. This is, according to Cassirer, an interdetermination that is different from association. Association simply leaves interdetermination unexplained.

At this point in his discussion, Cassirer distinguished his position from rationalistic as well as empiricist theories of knowledge (Figure 2.4).

In Cassirer's account, rationalistic theories aimed to save and demonstrate the independence of "meaning." Rationalistic theory confirmed Descartes' dictum that the unity of the objective world can be apprehended by perception, only through the reflection of the mind on itself (i.e., by *inspection menis*; *PSF* 3: 103). In contrast, we find the empiricist theory of association. Here Cassirer prepared his ground, claiming, "but it fails to overcome the inner tension between two fundamentally different elements of consciousness, between its mere 'matter' and its pure 'form'" (*PSF* 1: 103). Descartes' ideas of what Cassirer called "outward

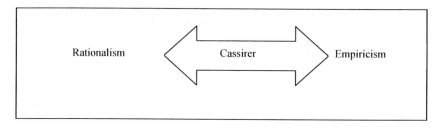

Figure 2.4 Cassirer between rationalism and empiricism.

perception" (e.g., lightness and darkness, roughness and smoothness, colored and resonant) are presented merely as subjective elements. But Cassirer sought to go beyond this stage, from the variability of impressions to the unity and constancy of the object. Doing so takes the function of judgment and what Cassirer called "unconscious inference," which is "totally independent of the impressions" (*PSF* 1: 104), but also molded by symbolic action.

FLUID IMPRESSIONS MOLDED BY SYMBOLIC ACTION

According to Cassirer, Descartes' metaphysical dualism is rooted in his methodological dualism (i.e., in a theory of absolute division between the substance of extension and the thinking substance). He also found this antithesis between sensibility and thought, material and formal determinants of consciousness, in the beginning of Kant's *Critique of Pure Reason* (first published in 1781). Cassirer defended Kant by pointing out that Kant after all opened the possibility that a stronger connection may exist between the two, based on common roots that are unknown to us.

In contrast with the empiricist idea of "association," Cassirer argued for "integration," as illustrated in Figure 2.5.

The elements of consciousness are closely related to the whole of consciousness, according to Cassirer. The nature of a content of consciousness "(. . .) exists only in so far as it immediately goes beyond itself in various directions of synthesis" (*PSF* 1: 104). We need to understand sensation and thought as integrated, not associated. Moments contain reference to temporal succession; a single point in space contains reference to space as the sum of all possible designations of position.

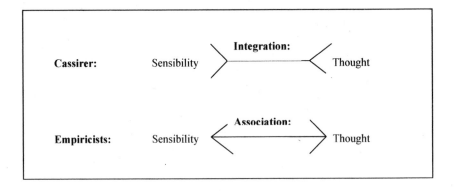

Figure 2.5   Integration versus association.

Cassirer developed a relational theory. Integration means relationship, and the relationship becomes necessary and immediately intelligible when it is considered from the standpoint of consciousness, he claimed:

> For here there is not from the very start an abstract 'one,' confronted with an equally abstract and detached 'other'; here the one is 'in' the many and the many is 'in' the one: in the sense that each determines and represents the other.
>
> (*PSF* 1: 105)

When Cassirer turned to the ideational content of the sign, he also clarified the relationship between the chaos of fluid sensory impressions and how they become clear and take form. "The fluid impression assumes form and duration for us only when we *mold* it by symbolic action in one direction or another" (*PSF* 1: 107). He illustrated how this "molding" takes different directions through different symbolic forms, a passage that is central in understanding the idea of symbolic forms:

> In science and language, in art and myth, this formative process proceeds in different ways and according to different principles, but all these spheres have this in common: that the product of their activity in no way resembles the mere *material* by which they began. It is in the basic symbolic function and its various directions that the spiritual consciousness and the sensory consciousness are first truly differentiated. It is here that we pass beyond passive receptivity to an indeterminate outward material, and begin to place upon it our independent imprint which articulates it for us into diverse spheres and forms of reality. Myth and art, language and science, are in this sense configurations *towards* being: they are not simple copies of an existing reality but represent the main directions of the spiritual movement, of the ideal process by which reality is constituted for us as one and many—as a diversity of forms which are ultimately held together by a unity of meaning.
>
> (*PSF* 1: 107)

Consciousness is representation and mediation. All forms of consciousness appear in the form of a temporal process; but in the course of the process, Cassirer claimed that certain types of "form" tend to detach themselves (PSF 1: 110). The different symbolic forms realize this universal tendency in different ways. Language, myth, art and science mediate differently through processes of symbolic pregnance[3] and form our channels to reality. The forms become background as well as foreground, as illustrated in Figure 2.6.

Cassirer understood the symbolic forms as "immediate forms of living" (*PSF* 1: 110). They are, at the same time, offering certain fixed points or resting places, and constantly renewing processes of consciousness. In the symbolic forms, consciousness retains a character of constant flux, articulated around certain fixed centers of form and meaning.

MODERN SCIENCE, VICO, AND POETIC KNOWLEDGE

In his chapter "Philosophical Idealism," Cassirer maintained that Plato's sharp boundary between the concept "as such" and its representations gradually tends to disappear through the history of logic and epistemology (*PSF* 1: 126). Cassirer's own philosophy is an expression of the relational, processual flux of consciousness where reality is mediated through forms. As Cassirer later promised in *An Essay on Man* (1944), an understanding of these mediation processes may offer us channels to a deeper understanding of reality, and to more realistic knowledge of the world. However, when modern science became a hallmark of enlightenment, knowledge became something that could be reached through deduction. Science is, according to Cassirer, oriented toward general relations and inferences, toward deductive combinations (*PSF* 1: 138). All true knowledge then consists in creating names and combining them into sentences and judgments. Truth and falsehood become attributes of language, and not attributes of things. Consequently, a spirit deprived of language would lack all power over these attributes and would be unable to distinguish the true and the false (*PSF* 1: 138).

As Cassirer stressed in *An Essay on Man* (1944), science is one of many symbolic forms, but a form that has gained an undisputed position and that Cassirer himself regarded as the utmost representation of man's development.

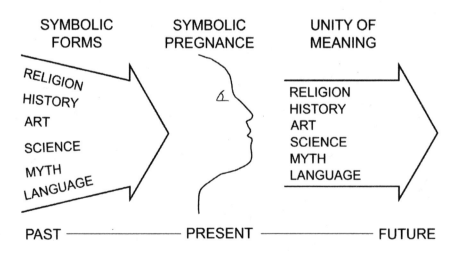

Figure 2.6   Symbolic forms and consciousness.

However, Cassirer endeavored to give an account of the different forms that are at hand for man. Man is characterized by the ability to choose angles of refraction, and the choices have distinct consequences. Science as a symbolic form is a channel to only certain parts of reality. Science reduces and classifies, inevitably implying an impoverishment of the world. It is an effective channel to the surface structures of the world; but as a means to achieve realistic knowledge, science as a single form of knowing is too restricted.

Not surprisingly, Cassirer turned to Vico in his discussion of alternative forms of knowledge. Giambattista Vico (1668–1744) was known as a stern combatant against Descartes. Vico claimed that Descartes' axioms could not be transferred to social science without problems. He built on Aristotle when he claimed that *phronesis* is a knowledge of a peculiar kind, an everyday knowledge that cannot be revealed by the means of scientific methods. This is a kind of "poetic wisdom," rather than universal truth, based on a *sensus communis*—a collective meaning and understanding that is not based on mathematics, but constructed through poetic language, contrary to Descartes' notion of reasoning. Fables, parables, metaphors, religion, pictures, and hieroglyphs are examples of how poetic knowledge was created.

Despite his admiration for Vico, Cassirer did point out that Vico posed the problem of language within the sphere of a general metaphysic of the spirit (*PSF* 1: 149), and therefore did not analyze consciousness as a result of symbolic understanding.[4] Cassirer seemed to use Vico and Vico's theory of language to pave the ground for his own theory of language as a symbolic form. In *An Essay on Man* (1944), he treated language (and, in a parallel way, science) as a way of gaining knowledge of reality, but a way that does not fully grasp the deepness and richness of reality and thus must be combined with other forms—art in particular—in order to achieve a realistic view the world.

ON SYMBOLIC FORMS AND THE PHILOSOPHICAL UNDERPINNINGS OF ORGANIZATIONAL THEORY

Cassirer's philosophy is indeed broad and ambitious, and commentators seem to disagree as to whether or not he was clear. Dimitry Gawronsky (1949), one of Cassirer's biographers, celebrated Cassirer's writing style and the way he presented his work:

> The most intricate philosophical problems are treated in a quite clear and simple way; one gets the impression that the author deeply felt his responsibility to truth and to the reader; in every sentence he sincerely tried to help the reader to advance on the thorny path of truth. Cassirer's style makes any subject he discusses almost transparent, and his argumentation glides along like a broad and mighty stream, with great convincing power.
>
> (Gawronsky 1949: 15)

Neher (2005) on the other hand criticized Cassirer as being sometimes vague and leaving much to the reader's imagination. However, Neher addressed possible reasons for Cassirer's lack of precision. One was that he did not want to limit his philosophical approach. "The 'Philosophy of Symbolic Forms' cannot and does not try to be a philosophical system in the traditional sense of this word" (Neher 2005: 364). Cassirer did not seek an overdetermination of the symbolic form's range of application, Neher claimed, and we are therefore left with a dynamic theory that is broad, and as such is open to new interpretations as new historical stages of consciousness bring forth new symbolic forms.

If Cassirer is broad and leaves much to the reader, as Neher maintains, the reader has to be conscious when it comes to what direction one wishes to take Cassirer. Cassirer has, for example, mistakenly been associated with current trends towards anti-intellectual intuitionism, antiscientific humanism, mysticism, and obscurantism, Nelson Goodman wrote in the opening page of his book *Ways of Worldmaking*. Then he tried to set things straight: "Actually these attitudes are as alien to Cassirer as to my own skeptical, analytic, contructionalist orientation" (Goodman 1978: 1).[5]

From my viewpoint of an educator; the following reasons have been particularly motivating when it comes to inquiry into Cassirer:

1. Particular historical circumstances forced Cassirer to leave Germany. One of the consequences of Cassirer's leaving was that the ongoing debate between the logical positivists of the Vienna circle and radical philosophy as represented by Heidegger came to an end. Another consequence was that when Cassirer left Europe, continental philosophy was left for Heidegger to dominate, whereas Anglo-Saxon philosophy became dominated by the analytic tradition.
2. Organizational theory seems to have been plagued by a split between two main schools, rooted in the philosophical underpinnings represented by the two main directions in philosophy.
3. Cassirer was not only a mediating force that facilitated a fruitful dialogue between the two schools, but through *The Philosophy of Symbolic Forms* and perhaps most clearly shown in *An Essay on Man* (1944), he developed a perspective that continued a trend lying before the split of the two schools.
4. Cassirer's writing style seems to reflect his interest in both science and art. He combined logical reasoning with literary writing and drew on examples from different art forms and a broad array of schools. Thus, reading Cassirer becomes a joyful experience.
5. Cassirer not only presents a philosophy, but also claims that taking his philosophy into action may turn one into a better practitioner.

The basic idea underpinning Cassirer's concept of Man as opposed to Animal is that we are capable of changing perspectives. Symbolic forms are examples of culturally developed perspectives (Neher 2005). Where Kant claimed that human reason finds itself in a realm of contradictions and darkness, Cassirer offered a more optimistic and proactive solution: through an understanding of symbolic forms and how the varying forms constitute our understanding of the world, man may enlarge his capacity to interact with the *real* world, to obtain a more *objective* view of the world. It is culturally and epistemologically a pluralistic perspective that leads to unified meaning, but it does not—and is not meant to—lead to solipsism or to radical relativism. Our understanding of the world is constituted by the various forms that, historically and culturally, are expressions of man's development of consciousness, but we are not confined within the borders of these forms. We are not merely, in a Heideggerian tradition, a spider that is incarcerated in its own web as an extension of itself, and we are not doomed to live in different incommensurable professional prisons where scholars are unable to communicate across paradigms (Burrell and Morgan 1979). It is through an understanding of the particularities of the various forms, the unity they constitute, as well as the ability to change perspectives where Cassirer pointed out a more optimistic and proactive solution.

3 Art and Science as Supplementing Forms

In this chapter, I concentrate on one of Cassirer's later works, *An Essay on Man* (1944). Here Cassirer discussed myth, language, science, religion, history, and art as symbolic forms, with special emphasis on the combination of the forms of art and science. According to Cassirer, science and art represent two views of truth that are distinctively different but at the same time supplementary channels to reality. Without the use of both the eye of science and the eye of art, we have no binocular vision and no awareness of the third dimension of space. Cassirer promised that the combination of these two forms may hinder habitual blindness and turn us into better practitioners. After Cassirer, the ways parted, and today we have two very different camps in organization theory.

CONDENSING THE MESSAGE AND TURNING TO PRACTICE

In the three volumes of *The Philosophy of Symbolic Forms,* Cassirer outlined a philosophy that suggested a combination of the scientific and the nonscientific. Here he concentrated on the symbolic forms of myth, language, and science. As an educator of managers and a student of organizations, my primary interest and motivation for writing this book is the application of Cassirer's philosophy in organization theory and how to develop better organizational practitioners. I will therefore turn to one of Cassirer's later and most practical works, *An Essay on Man* (1944). Cassirer wrote this book in English as an introduction of his philosophy of symbolic forms to the American audience. As such, it is both a condensation and an extension of his major ideas. Here he both clarified and simplified the central thoughts he had presented in *The Philosophy of Symbolic Forms,* and he discussed their practical consequences. Thus, the reader escapes some of the vagueness that was present in *The Philosophy of Symbolic Form.* In *An Essay on Man,* he also expanded examples of the forms. He still dealt with myth, language, and science, as he had done twenty years earlier, but here he added religion, history, and art to the list.[1]

Cassirer was forced to leave Germany in 1933 when the Nazis came to power. He was by then at the University of Hamburg, where he was its first Jewish rector. He lectured at Oxford University until 1935 (first spending about three months learning the English language) and then moved to Sweden when he became a professor at Gothenburg University (where he also learned Swedish in a short time). In 1941, he moved to the U.S., where he lectured at Yale University until moving to Columbia University in New York in 1943. He then lectured at Columbia until his death in 1945.

As Friedman (2000) pointed out, Cassirer's philosophy lost momentum due to historical circumstances. Heidegger could dominate continental Europe, and analytic philosophy took the U.S. and England. In other words, Cassirer's impact may seem mediocre: although he was one of the most prominent scholars of the Weimar Republic, he seems to have gotten lost between two dominating and antagonistic traditions.

However, to say that Cassirer had no heritage would be to draw too simple a picture. Among Cassirer's students were Suzanne Langer, Kurt Lewin, Emmanuel Levinas, and Erwin Panofsky. Langer is remembered for building on Cassirer in her work on the symbol and introducing his ideas to literary and aesthetic audiences. Lewin became known as the founder of Action Research, and built on Cassirer when he developed his force field analysis.[2] Levinas developed the ethics of "the Other," and Panofsky is known as one of the foremost art historians. But Cassirer also influenced others, including Herbert Blumer, who introduced "symbolic interactionism," and Russian author and philosopher Mikhail Bakhtin to the point that Bakhtin was accused of plagiarism (Poole and Hitchcock 1998), as well as Goodman's theory of "worldmaking" (Goodman 1978). And, of course, others seem to have been influenced by Cassirer as well, even though they may have differed from and disagreed with Cassirer in many important regards; examples are John Dewey, Michel Foucault (suggested by Østerberg 2002), Martin Buber, and George Lakoff.

In the last few decades, it is probably in the works of the French sociologist and philosopher Pierre Bourdieu that we find the strongest influence, especially when it comes to how *habitus* as a culturally developed predisposition mediates the relationship between the individual and society. Bourdieu (1990) recognized Cassirer as one of the most important inspirations for his own work.

Despite Cassirer's strong position before the Second World War and some distinguished scholars who have carried the torch, the momentum he achieved became lost along the way due to historical circumstances. In particular, Cassirer's philosophy seems to have had very limited influence on organizational theory.

The rationale should be strong for considering Cassirer as an alternative to the current divide between analytic and interpretative schools in organizational theory. This piece of writing is my modest attempt to understand the philosophy of symbolic forms and its potential relevance to organizational theory and management education. Because its potential application is my main inspiration, I will now concentrate on Cassirer's discussion of science (which he sometimes parallels with language) and art. Cassirer promised that we will become better practitioners if we succeed in combining science and art. However, later commentators largely overlooked the connection he made between these two. In this chapter, I will therefore turn to *An Essay on Man,* which was published in 1944, only one year prior to his death.

MAN AS ANIMAL SYMBOLICUM

The notion of man as an *animal symbolicum* is central in *An Essay on Man* (1944). In our modern world, we tend to see ourselves as an *animal rationale,* Cassirer claimed. Instead, he proposed that we would benefit from understanding man as a symbolic animal. Man lives in a world of signs and symbols. Symbols, in the proper sense of the term, cannot be reduced to mere signals. Signals and symbols belong to two different universes of discourse: a signal is part of the physical world of being, and a symbol is part of the human world of meaning. Signals are "operators"; symbols are "designators." Signals, even when understood and used as such, have nevertheless a sort of physical or substantial being, whereas symbols have only a functional value, according to Cassirer.

To illustrate his point, Cassirer used the examples of Pavlov's dogs, and Clever Hans, a horse that (according to his owner) responded to questions requiring mathematical calculations by tapping his hoof. Through these examples, Cassirer demonstrated how an animal possesses a practical imagination and intelligence, whereas man alone has developed the new form of *symbolic imagination and intelligence.* Cassirer also made use of the legendary Helen Keller (1880–1968) to demonstrate the mental development of the individual mind from one form to another (from a merely practical attitude to a symbolic attitude). The story of this blind deaf-mute's journey to a communicative community exemplifies how the symbolic function of words can open a new horizon, a wider and freer area in which to roam, according to Cassirer. Everything has a name, and the symbolic function is a principle of universal applicability that encompasses the whole field of human thought. To Helen Keller, this discovery came as a sudden shock: the child began to see the world in a new light.

Thus, the principle of symbolism became Cassirer's magic word, the "Open Sesame!" He claimed that symbolism has its own universality, validity, and general applicability, giving access to that which is specifically of the human world (i.e., to the world of human culture).[3] Once man is in possession of this magic key, further progress is guaranteed. Such progress is evidently not hindered or made impossible by any lack in the material sense, as shown in the case of Helen Keller. Human beings in the construction of their human world are not dependent on the quality of their sense material, Cassirer asserted; they can construct their symbolic world out of the poorest and scantiest material. This process of construction is also a process of reflection, which becomes an important capacity to single out from the whole indiscriminate mass or the stream of floating sensuous phenomena certain fixed elements in order to separate them and to direct attention upon them. Cassirer showed how the loss or impairment of speech caused by brain injury alters the ability to reflect and thus the whole character of human behavior, as shown in the study of the psychopathology of language. Such changes are seldom apparent in the patients' outward behavior. They tend to act in a perfectly normal manner. They can perform the tasks of everyday life; some can even build substantial skills, but they are at a complete loss as soon as the problem requires any specific theoretical or reflective activity, Cassirer claimed. They are no longer able to think in general concepts or categories. Having lost their grip on universals, they are glued to immediate facts and concrete situations. The ability to reflect is lost. Accordingly, the crucial ability to differentiate between the "real" and the "possible" is also lost. Like animals, one is then confined to the world of sense perceptions.

Cassirer claimed that empiricists and positivists have always maintained that the utmost mission of human knowledge is to give us the facts and nothing but the facts. However, human knowledge is by its very nature symbolic knowledge. A symbol has no actual existence as a part of the physical world: it has a "meaning." Language, art, myth, religion, science, and history are examples of systems of human activities and outstanding characteristics of man's work. They are, in Cassirer's terminology, symbolic forms that represent different perspectives that can be taken of any object. Accordingly, science alone does not provide us with a sufficient channel to reality. It has to be complemented by other forms of understanding, and in *An Essay on Man*, Cassirer specifically emphasized *art* as a supplement to science. Art leads to a more realistic view of things and life, he maintained. It is a way for us to discover the external world, but not in the same way as we do through science.

SCIENCE, ART, AND THE THIRD DIMENSION OF SPACE

Science's way to the objective world is through classification of our sense perceptions, according to Cassirer. Science and language help us ascertain and determine our concepts of the external world to give them meaning. Such classification is the result of a determined effort toward simplification. In contrast, art is an act of condensation and concentration. "Language and science are abbreviations of reality; art is an intensification of reality" (Cassirer 1944: 143). Art is not just a reproduction or imitation of a ready-made, given reality; rather, it is a discovery of reality through a continuous process of concentration.

Cassirer saw man as an animal that has discovered a new method of adapting himself to the environment. Building on the biologist Jakob von Uexküll (1864–1944),[4] he illustrated how every organism, even the lowest, possesses a certain *Merknetz* or receptor system, and a certain *Wirknetz* or effector system. These two systems cooperate and strive towards equilibrium. Through the receptor system, the organism receives outward stimuli; through the effector system, it reacts to those stimuli. These processes are closely interwoven as links in the same chain that Uexküll called the *Funktionskreis*, or the functional circle of the animal.

The functional circle of man has undergone a qualitative change, according to Cassirer. In addition to the receptor system and the effector system, which are to be found in all animal species, man has developed a third link, the *symbolic system*. In contrast with other animals, man lives not simply in a broader reality; he lives in a new dimension of reality. However, this dimension is gradually taken out of sight through habitual ways of unilateral concentration on the formal structures of life, as well as a preoccupation with causality and finality (i.e., through using "the eye of science and language" alone). To grasp the richness of the world, we need art as a special direction or an orientation for our thoughts, feelings, and imagination. In the realm of art, Cassirer maintained, we forget to ask "What is that for?" or "Where does that come from?" Instead, we discover the forms of things behind their empirical properties. In this sense, art is not merely a way of identifying static elements (e.g., ornaments, accessories, or embellishments), according to Cassirer, but a way of revealing the mobile order and a new horizon of nature.

Art and science move in completely different planes, and they cannot oppose or avoid each other, Cassirer maintained. In our attempts to uncover the theoretical reasons or the practical effects of things, we concentrate on causality or finality, Cassirer claimed. The consequence is that we habitually lose sight of their instant appearances. We then develop a sort of blindness. The role of art is to teach us to visualize, and not only conceptualize or utilize, things. Art provides us with a richer, more vivid and colorful representation of reality, as well as a more profound insight into the formal structures of reality. By using "the eye of science as well as the eye of art" simultaneously, we come closer to the third dimension of space and to a more realistic view of our world, Cassirer seems to promise.

ART IS KNOWLEDGE

Cassirer asserted that like all the other symbolic forms, art is not the mere replica of a ready-made, prearranged reality, but one of the ways leading to a more realistic view of things and of human life. It is not an imitation but a discovery of reality. We do not, however, discover nature through art in the same sense in which the scientist uses the term "nature." Through language and science, we establish and determine our concepts of the external world, according to Cassirer. It is a process of abstraction, as illustrated in Figure 3.1

We must classify our sense perceptions to provide them an objective meaning. Such classification is the consequence of a persistent attempt to simplify. Language and science depend on the same process of abstraction, whereas art may be explained as a continuous process of concretion. "The artist is just as much a discoverer of the forms of nature as the scientist is a discoverer of facts or natural laws" (Cassirer 1944: 143–144).

Cassirer used the work of artists to illustrate how one may achieve deeper insight through the artistic process. He depicted painters and sculptors as the experts in the territory of the visible world. Their awareness of pure forms of things is not an instinctive gift of nature; it can be learned. What we need is to "open the artistic eye." A certain blindness gradually develops and becomes habitual. We thus may have encountered an object of our usual sense experience numerous times without ever having "seen" its form. We become bewildered if asked to describe not its physical qualities or effects, but its pure visual shape and structure. Art fills this gap, Cassirer alleged. We live, however, in a world of science occupied with the analysis and scrutiny of sense objects and the study of their effects. But science means abstraction, and abstraction is always an impoverishment of reality. Cassirer wrote, "Aesthetic experience is incomparably richer" (1944: 149). The great painters show us the form of external things. The great dramatists show us the form of inner life. Dramatic art discloses a new breadth and depth of life. Art offers an awareness of human things and human fates, of human immensity and despair, by comparison. Thus, we need art to provide us this intensification and illumination, following Cassirer.

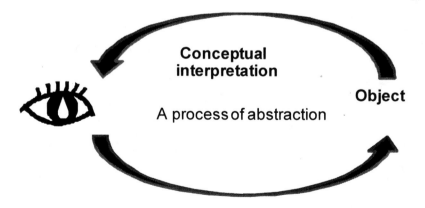

Figure 3.1 The eye of science as conceptual interpretation.

The degree of intensification and illumination is the measure of the excellence of art. The art process brings us new insight, a light of consciousness, when the artist, the spectator, and the auditors interact. Like the process of speech, the artistic process is dialogical and dialectic. Not even the spectator is left to a purely passive role. We cannot understand a work of art without, to a certain degree, repeating and reconstructing the creative process by which it has come into being, according to Cassirer.

Consequently, art brings insights into deeper layers of reality. Cassirer believed that awareness of the depth of things always requires an effort on the part of our productive energies. One should then be aware that artistic and scientific energies do not move in the same direction, he held forth. They do not tend toward the same end; thus, they cannot provide us the same aspect of reality. Conceptual depth is discovered by science and focuses on discovering the reason of things. Purely visual depth is revealed in art and focuses on seeing their forms. In science, we try to trace phenomena back to their first causes, to general laws and principles. In art, we are absorbed in the phenomena's immediate appearance, Cassirer maintained; we are not concerned about the uniformity of laws but about the multiformity and diversity of intuitions.

A central assertion in Cassirer's philosophy is that science and art represent two views of truth that are in contrast with one another, but not in conflict or contradiction. It is the nature of man not to be limited to one specific and single approach to reality but to choose a point of view. Accordingly, art is knowledge, but it is knowledge of a peculiar and specific kind.

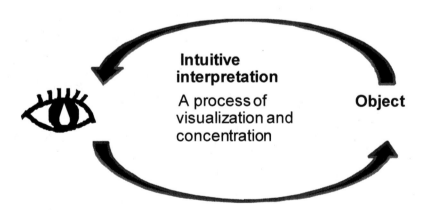

Figure 3.2   The eye of art as intuitive interpretation.

THE LOGIC OF THE HUMANITIES AS THE
LOGIC OF THE EYE OF ART

If it is the natural sciences that most evidently provide the logic, the level of refraction, and the values of the eye of science, where should we turn in order to fully understand the eye of art? An obvious first answer would be to the arts themselves. However, art is, as in the case of physics and biology, part of a larger tradition. Whereas physics and biology are subcategories of science, art is a discipline within the broader category of the humanities.

If one intends to understand the logic of the eye of art, it would not be sufficient to study specific forms of visual or performing arts. Studying dance, for example, or music, will certainly reveal a lot about art, just as analyzing herpetology or ornithology will reveal information about science. However, in order to fully understand science, you will have to look for its general tendencies, preferences, and logics. Accordingly, in order to understand the eye of art, you will have to turn to the specificities of the humanities and how these characteristics make the humanities different from science.[5]

Having previously analyzed the natural sciences in *Substance and Function* (Cassirer 1910),[6] Cassirer in *Logic of the Humanities*[7] ([1942] 1961)[8] undertakes a non-dualistic analysis of the humanities. In the forward, his translator Clarence Smith Howe states that Cassirer's Logic of the Humanities is " . . . an analysis of those basic concepts which underlie our arts, our knowledge of history, and our disciplined knowledge of human nature", where "the value of a study of these concepts and their interrelationships" is that

> . . . it enables us to see more in a work of art, or in our direct encounter with human personality, than we otherwise would. It is the study of disciplined perception, whether of the eye or the ear; as such, it is a logic of concrete universal. This concreteness, directness, and wholeness are precisely what distinguish the logic of the humanities from the traditional logic of abstract universals. (Howe 1961: xiv)

Cassirer first defined his concept of symbolic form in a 1923 essay called "*Der Begriff der symbolischen Form im Aufbau der Geisteswissenschaften*," or "*The Concept of the Symbolic Form in the Formation of the Humanities*" (Krois 2009). The title indicates what is to become central in Cassirer's philosophy: *Symbolism*. The principle of symbolism is what makes us truly human; it is what both creates and opens the human world to us, allowing us to roam in a world of human culture. Access to this "magic key" is a necessity for further progress and liberation. It is a process of construction, a worldmaking process as Goodman (1978) probably would have said, giving us access to the cultures' universals when at the same time we become cocreators of the same universals. These universals help us, as Cassirer writes in *Logic of the Humanities* (1961), transcend "the multiplicity and diversity of momentary impressions" by establishing, gradually and by stages, a "stability," and "common cosmos" that is determinate (*LoH*: 60). By taking part of a culture by means of the key of symbolism, we become cocreators of these universals, exemplified by Cassirer in the symbolic form of language:

> What we call "learning" a language is, accordingly, never a purely receptive or reproductive process, but one that is productive in the highest degree. In this process the ego not only gains insight into an enduring order but shares in constructing it. For the ego does not win its share in this order by simply joining itself to it, as to something present and given; instead, it gains its share in it [only through the process by which, and] as each particular, each individual, acquires order, and it contributes to the maintenance and renewal of this order in and by virtue of this [process of] acquisition. (*LoH*: 60)

The key of symbolism takes man to a world of meaning, interpretation, values, and culture. This is the playground of the humanities. In *Logic of the Humanities,* Cassirer takes on a cultural interpretation of mind and self, and he does so under the influence of the attempts by Dilthey and his followers, according to his translator Clarence Smith Howe (1961: xii). The tradition represented by Dilthey is the German interpretive tradition of *Geisteswissenschaften* or *Kulturwissenschaften*,[9] which, following Howe, should not be understood as "the social sciences," but rather as the humanities (Howe 1961: xiii–xiv).

If we are to take Cassirer's challenge seriously, and strive to understand the world by combining the eye of art and the eye of science, we should, accordingly, turn to the humanities if one needs to strengthen the eye of art. The humanities may help us understand how a " . . . life of 'meanings' supplants the life of mere impulses" (*LoH*: 60).

These meanings must be understood not as a stripped here-and-now, but rather in the light of recurring and repeating life-moments and in the misuse and use of innumerable other persons, Cassirer holds forth. In order to fully understand our reality, we will have to understand facts in a historical and cultural perspective. As Cassirer puts it, to give " . . . historical order and interpretation to a fact is to relate it to universal values" (*LoH*: 90). Making sense and creating meaning is a process here-and-now, but this here-and-now process must be understood in a larger picture:

> Like every other object, an object of culture has its place in space and time. It has it's here-and-now. It comes to be and passes away. Insofar as we describe this here-and-now, this coming-to-be and passing-away, we have no need to go beyond the sphere of physical determinants. But, on the other hand, in this description even the physical itself is seen in

a new function. It not only "is" and "becomes"; for in this being and becoming something else "emerges." What emerges is a "meaning," which is not absorbed by what is merely physical, but is embodied upon and within it; it is the factor common to all that content which we designate as "culture." To be sure, nothing prevents us from ignoring this factor, making us blind to its "symbolic value" through such a leaving-out and overlooking mode of abstraction. *(LoH: 98)*

"Nothing prevents us from ignoring this factor, making us blind to its 'symbolic value' through such a leaving-out and overlooking mode of abstraction," Cassirer concludes. As I hope to show in this book, this seems to be just what we have done in the dominant organizational theories and our teaching of management, unfortunately.

A CALL FOR BINOCULAR VISION

I have not found that Cassirer directly explained why he chose to discuss the importance of combining art and science in particular, among all the symbolic forms he investigated. Why not art in combination with history? Or myth and language? My guess is that that these two forms and their relationship to each other became increasingly essential in both Cassirer's philosophy and in his own life. They illustrate the mediating role that Cassirer came to play throughout his academic life and the ongoing debates he facilitated and stimulated between science and the humanities. Epistemologically, the two forms of science and art also seem to illustrate particularly well Cassirer's attempt to establish a non-dualistic philosophy that does not deny man's capacity to reach a more realistic and objective world.

When Cassirer analyzed the logics of science, he did so based on the natural sciences (Naturwissenschaften) as an ideal form; and he gradually developed his ideas of a relationship between the natural sciences and its counterview, the humanities (*Geisteswissenschaften*), which Cassirer sometimes called the cultural sciences *(Kulturwissenschaft)*.[10] Therefore, his discussion of art versus science in *An Essay on Man* in all probability reflects his long-time interest in exploring the relationship between science and the humanities. My supposition is that Cassirer found that the combination of the two forms of art and science had epistemological consequences that were particularly easy to explain to his new audience. The peculiarities of art and science seem to be well suited as an illustration of the usefulness of his philosophy. That is, his combination of these two specific forms was not only driven by his mediating role between the major traditions of what was to become known as Anglo-Saxon analytic and continental radical traditions, but also by an interest in reaching a new audience. By exemplifying the epistemological consequences of art versus science, he explored and explained how we interrelate with the external world and how we may gain knowledge that can bring us closer to reality and make us better at navigating in what he called three-dimensional space.

By bringing in art as a symbolic form, Cassirer forcefully and beautifully pointed to the power of artistic imagination and how we relate to the world through the logic that follows art as a symbolic form. Art is a way of "being and acting in the world," where quality depends on the ability to illuminate the multilevel world. In that respect, Cassirer's view of the role of art differs from, for example, Lotte Darsø's (2004) otherwise thorough presentation of art-in-business. Darsø claimed that arts-in-business involved four basic options for the use of art: for decoration, for entertainment, as instruments (e.g., for teambuilding, communication training, and innovation), or in integration with the strategic processes of transformation. Darsø described *different functions* of art in organizations. Art becomes an object, a tool, or a technique rather than a way of approaching, seeing, sensing, understanding, creating, and acting.

Like teachers of innovative management classes, business seems more and more to apply art as technique. But critical voices are also heard from the art-in-business camp. Daved Barry was one such critic:

> How does one think of such [creative] projects? The old view would have us think of muses and other out-of-the-blue, knock-on-the-head things. A newer one stemming from social psychology (Amabile 1996) would suggest that simply asking oneself (or others) to be creative can be enough. But I don't think either one of these can get us to artfully creative ideas. Too often the many creativity techniques that are around result in a mechanical otherness, something that is different, but not lifefully so.
>
> (Barry 2008: 38)

In the Aristotelian tradition, one might say that Darsø primarily depicted art as *techne,* whereas Cassirer explored art as a practical form of knowing that was different from both *techne* and *episteme,* the latter understood as a form of knowing usually related to science. Art as aesthetic knowing became in Cassirer's philosophy a channel to the world with practical consequences, and as such it was closer to Aristotle's *phronesis.*

Cassirer's approach was thus more profound than the use of art as *techne,* in the sense that he presented art as a form of knowing and a way of attaining a more objective view of the world. Taken into organizations, art consequently should open the eye that makes it possible for us to go beyond the formal structures of organizational life. Together with science, art makes it possible to develop a three-dimensional view of organizations, if we are to believe Cassirer. For example, all of the four functions of art-in-business described by Darsø may be understood in both scientific and artistic ways; but the combined use of the symbolic forms of art *and* science, when understanding these and other organizational phenomena, makes it possible to understand how the surface and deeper levels interact. This seems to me to be the core of Cassirer's practical message: we need to develop the capacity to cope with the world in a binocular way by combining the forms of science and art.

Applied to organizations, art is not primarily a question of metaphors, decoration, entertainment, or tools for achieving something, although art may also fill all these functions. In Cassirer's landscape, art is more than function: it is about how we relate to, interact with, and shape the world. It is about intensifying more than reducing, creating rather than categorizing. But Cassirer was not an ambassador of art alone. Science is still an important way of grasping the world. Cassirer perceived science as the last step in man's mental progress, and the highest and most characteristic realization of human culture. Nonetheless, science is not sufficient. Being a competent practitioner requires the use of both eyes instead of merely one; it requires the eye of science and language as well as the eye of art. Without this binocular vision, we lose insight into what Cassirer regarded as the third dimension of space, which should apply to the space of organizing as well.

MANAGEMENT KNOWLEDGE BEYOND THE SURFACE LEVEL

Cassirer illustrated how Kant presented the difference between the real and the possible as a characteristic of man, the distinctiveness of the human intellect, the character of human knowledge that distinguishes man from other beings. This difference does not exist for beings below or above human beings, according to Kant. The superhuman divine mind (used by Kant merely as illustration) does not make a distinction between what is and what is not: everything is real for the divine. On the level beneath man, animals are confined within their world of sense perceptions. It is characteristic of man, and of man alone, to live in a world of actuality and possibility at the same time. This is an epistemological difference, not a metaphysical difference, according to Cassirer. The human mind is based on a "discursive understanding" that depends on two different elements: we are not able to think without images, and we are not able to intuit without concepts, according to Kant: "Concepts without intuitions are empty, intuitions without concepts are blind" (*EoM*: 56). This dualism underlies the distinction between possibility and actuality.

Cassirer asserted that this passage is one of the most important and most difficult in Kant's critical works. However, Cassirer felt the need to reformulate Kant. Instead of claiming that the human intellect is "in need of images," Cassirer proposed that we should say human intellect is in need of *symbols*. "Human knowledge is by its very nature symbolic knowledge" (*EoM*: 57). Here Cassirer made his ground for a demarcation between Kant and himself. Both the strength and the limitation of the human intellect lie in the fact that human knowledge is symbolic knowledge, and it is this distinctiveness that makes man capable of distinguishing between the actual and the ideal world, between the real and the possible.

Applying Cassirer to the education of managers[11] and the development of organizational expertise seems to imply certain consequences. First, an education that builds on a set of scientific thought alone may, in the reduction and impoverishment that inevitably follows categorization and classification, lose its imaginative and creative force and contribute to a progressive habitual blindness that makes us increasingly unaware of the deeper levels of organizations. The ability to see "what is still not here" and "what is not on the surface" may be lost. This fact takes us once again back to Cassirer's claim that we need to develop the capacity to see with "both eyes." In order to be powerful, an education thus has to combine a scientific form of knowing (i.e., the symbolic form of science) with an aesthetic awareness and the logics and levels of refraction that follow the symbolic form of art. Developing management expertise thus requires that we transgress the historically developed dichotomy between different forms of knowing—not in order to merge them, but to recognize and utilize their complementary qualities. Needless to say, doing so raises several problems, such as determining which schools of interpretive theory represent the required supplementary qualities. Because, according to Cassirer, science takes us to the surface structures, to language and symbols, it follows that we should choose to supplement science with schools that have the capacity to go *beyond* surface structures. Here we encounter difficulties with "hard" social constructivist, postmodern, poststructural schools that either claim that the text is all there is, as well as "softer" versions that claim even if an absolute reality does exist, we have no way of knowing reality and therefore are confined within the limits of language. The irony is that the most radical schools, in their opposition to positive science, also restrict us to the surface level of reality. The consequence of radical schools as well as positive science is that our channel to the world stops where language stops, and we run out of concepts.

CASSIRER AS A STARTING POINT FOR RECONCILIATION?

Cassirer saw art and science as two symbolic forms that represent distinctively different but supplementary channels to reality. That is, they represent two different paths to, and ways of organizing, the same reality. They lead us to different layers of reality, but the combination of these two forms may have the most important epistemological and practical consequences.

Cassirer fell between different poles and, in particular, between the poles of *Naturwissenschaften* and *Geisteswissenschaften*. Cassirer was difficult to categorize because he represented a third relational alternative when he argued against (but also was inspired by) Heidegger's radical phenomenology as well as the Vienna circle of logical empiricists. However, when Cassirer left Germany, that third alternative disappeared. Since that time, it seems that philosophy in general (Friedman 2000; Friedman 2005) and organizational theory in particular (Barry and Hansen 2008; Fiol and O'Connor 2008; Martin 2003) have continued and reinforced this antagonism. The rational approaches of organization theory and management science—with a focus on concrete surface phenomena with formal plans, quantitative objectives, and hierarchical organizational structures—now stand in sharp contrast to the interpretative views of organization as deep-level phenomena with values, norms, interpretations, feelings, and mental images as the main areas of interest. The ontological and epistemological assumptions underlying these two directions represent different views of knowledge as "truth" and as "thing" versus "process" and "relations" (Hamlin, Keep, and Ash 2001; Newell, Robertson, Scarbrough, and Swan 2002). The consequence of the parting of the ways seems to be two main camps in management theory and practice. In its simplest version, management becomes programming and control; or it becomes adaptation, exploration, learning, and symbolic management. Cassirer challenged us to overcome this dualism.

Michael Friedman (2000) asked where should one start in beginning a reconciliation of the analytic and continental traditions. After a thorough analysis, he identified in his book *A Parting of the Ways: Carnap, Cassirer, and Heidegger* the weaknesses in both the radical school (represented by Martin Heidegger) and the analytic school (represented by the logical positivist Rudolph Carnap) and ended up recommending the less-known Ernst Cassirer. "(One) can find no better starting point than the rich treasure of ideas, ambitions, and analysis stored in his astonishingly comprehensive body of philosophical work" (Friedman 2000: 159).

ON THE PARTING OF THE WAYS IN PHILOSOPHY

In the late 1920s, positivism was most significantly represented by the Vienna Circle, with such influential names as Moritz Schlick (1882–1936), Otto Neurath (1882–1945), and Rudolph Carnap (1891–1970). Their "logical positivism" (also known as neo-positivism) was based on a strong belief in experience as the only source of knowledge and in the use of logical analysis as the preferred method of clarification of philosophical problems. When Carnap moved to the U.S. in 1935, he became an important contributor to the advancement of the American tradition often called analytic (or scientific) philosophy, which in turn contributed to the functionalistic traditions in organization theory that, according to Mintzberg (2004) and Ghoshal (2005), have been dominant in American business schools and that, according to Czarniawska (2003), have achieved hegemony in the management curricula in large parts of the Western world.

The development of the interpretive tradition (also known as romantic, idealistic, relativistic, constructivist, and postmodern) can be understood as a reaction against the dominance of the natural sciences. This reaction came from the social sciences and the humanities in general, and from hermeneutic and phenomenological philosophy in particular. Friedrich Schleiermacher (1768–1834), Wilhelm Dilthey (1833–1911), and Emilio Betti (1890–1968) were among the contributors to classic hermeneutics, whereas Hans Georg Gadamer (1900–2002) stood out as one of the most distinctive representatives of late hermeneutics.

At the beginning of the twentieth century, hermeneutic philosophy took a phenomenological turn towards the analysis of consciousness and towards epistemological questions with the works of Edmund Husserl (1859–1938). Husserl's student Martin Heidegger (1889–1976) moved phenomenological philosophy toward a more radical and relativistic direction. Partially for historical and social reasons, Heidegger achieved a hegemonic status as the most prominent continental philosopher after the Second World War:

> In Europe, by contrast, the only truly major philosopher left was Heidegger himself, and it is no wonder, then, that what we now call the continental tradition invariably takes its starting point from him. And it was only at this particular point that the two traditions became thoroughly estranged, to the point of almost total mutual incomprehension, linguistically, geographically, and conceptually.
>
> (Friedman 2000: 157)

Analytic (or scientific) philosophy advanced in the U.S. and England and fueled the tradition in organization theory that now has been so strongly criticized by Mintzberg (2004), Czarniawska (2003), and Ghoshal (2005); meanwhile, European continental philosophy became dominated by Heidegger, who had a major influence on the later expansion of relativistic directions such as deconstruction, poststructuralism, and postmodernism—directions that stand as antagonistic and seemingly incommensurable counterparts to functionalistic organizational theories.[12]

However, until the Nazi party came to power, the positivistic and continental schools were not estranged. Before the ways parted, a common dialogue and interaction occurred between the representatives of the different schools, as described by Michael Friedman (2000). Friedman specifically analyzed a meeting that took place in the spring of 1929 in Davos, Switzerland. Martin Heidegger, who had just completed his main work *Zein und Seit* (*Being and Time* (first published in 1927)), was to present a series of lectures together with Ernst Cassirer, at that time a leading philosopher in Germany. The Vienna Circle logical positivist Rudolph Carnap, who in 1928 had published *The Logical Structure of the World*, also took part in this three-week intensive international university course.[13]

CASSIRER VERSUS HEIDEGGER

The meeting between 17 March and 6 April 1929, the second of a series of seminars called *Davoser Hochschulkurse,* is sometimes described in an almost mythical way. It is illustrative how Skidelsky opens his book on Cassirer:

> On the one side was Ernst Cassirer, distinguished representative of the German idealist tradition and champion of the Weimar Republic. On the other was Martin Heidegger, the younger man, whose recently published *Being and Time* had shaken the idealist tradition to its foundations, and whose politics, though still uncertain, were plainly far from liberal. It was a symbolic moment. The old was pitted against the new, the humanism of the eighteenth and nineteenth centuries against the radicalism of the twentieth. All agreed that Heidegger, not Cassirer, was the man of the future. No one realized just what that future held in store. (Skidelsky 2008: 1)

One of Cassirer's biographers, Massimo Ferrari (2003), depicted it as a meeting where not only the future of philosophy was at play, but also as a meeting where two unlike personalities confronted one another and where anti-Semitism also played a role. However, Thomas Meyer (2006), another Cassirer biographer, depicted Heidegger and Cassirer as indeed unlike in many ways, but also as respectful and polite towards each other. Heidegger, in a letter to his friend Elisabeth Blochman after the meeting, actually complained that Cassirer was too *vornehm,* too noble and polite, in their discussions and offered too little resistance for a sharp discussion to take place (Meyer 2006: 172). Cassirer's demeanor can perhaps be explained both by his gentle manner and by his positive attitude toward parts of Heidegger's works. Meyer also maintained that Cassirer felt "positively challenged" by Heidegger, and had read Heidegger's *Zein und Seit* with great interest. Cassirer used his lectures in Davos to illustrate and discuss where he and Heidegger shared common grounds and where they parted. He addressed topics central to Heidegger (e.g., time and space and death), whereas Heidegger took Kant as his point of departure.

However, albeit Cassirer had a gentle manner, genuine interest in, and admiration of Heidegger's works, it seems that he also clearly saw the radical and problematic consequences of Heidegger's ideas. Among the unpublished papers that John Michael Krois and Donald Phillip Verene edited and translated for the first time and that were published in 1996 as *The Philosophy of Symbolic Forms Volume 4* (from now on abbreviated *PSF 4*), we find Cassirer's notes on Heidegger's conception of "Geist" and "Life" in Being and Time. Here Cassirer writes, "He does not seek to derive the region of the geist from 'nature'—the ontology of existence from the being of 'things', from reality. On the contrary, he recognizes that this whole world of things, the world of 'reality', is a secondary phenomenon" (*PSF* 4: 201). Here we find the root of Heidegger's' "Idealism"; Cassirer holds forth and points to how Heidegger in Being and Time denies the existence of the world as long as there is no 'dasein.' The world according to Heidegger is neither present-at-hands nor ready-at-hand, it just temporalizes itself in temporality. A marginal note made by Cassirer in Being and Time is worth noticing: "Also especially 277: 'Because the kind of being that is essential to truth is of the character of Dasein, all truth is relative to Dasein's Being.'— This is dubious!—Cassirer."

It seems clear from these notes that Cassirer was fully aware of the radical relativistic consequences of Heidegger's position, and where he and Heidegger's ways parted. The following sequences are worth quoting in full:

> Everything "general", all giving in to the general is for Heidegger a "fall"—a disregarding of "authentic" *dasein*—a giving in to the inauthenticity of the "they" [*das "Man"*].
>
> Here, essentially, is where there is a parting of the ways between his path and ours. The ontologically cannot be separated from the ontic nor the individual from the "general" in the way that Heidegger tries to—rather, the one is only from within the other. (*PSF* 4: 201–202)

And here is where Cassirer's philosophy of the symbolic forms comes in:

> We understand the general not as the mere they, but as "objective spirit and objective culture". For Heidegger, thought has no access to such objectivity. So even the *logos,* language, now becomes a merely social phenomenon which as such—similar to Bergson—carries no genuine intelligent content. (*PSF* 4: 202)

A consequence of Heidegger's position is that discourse becomes only "talk about," Cassirer continues, it becomes superficial idle talk, and giving in to the general world is just seen as a way of looking away from oneself and a "fall from grace":

> Here, basically, is where we depart from him, because for us objective spirit is not exhausted by nor does it degenerate into the structure of everydayness. The "impersonal" does not consist merely in the pale, diluted social form of the average, the everydayness of the "they," but in the form of transpersonal meaning. For this transpersonal, Heidegger's philosophy has no access. (*PSF* 4: 202)

Cassirer admits that Heidegger has a perspective on history, but this historical understanding becomes merely repetition, repetition of personal aspects such as personal dasein, personal destinies, and personal fate. These perspectives are very well understood by Heidegger, according to Cassirer, but they are limited to what Cassirer calls a religious-individualistic comprehension of history. Meaning is to Cassirer more than personal meaning: "History as the history of culture, the history of meaning, as the life of the objective spirit is *not* thereby disclosed" (*PSF* 4: 203). A consequence of neglecting the role of the objective in culture will inevitably lead to blindness: "Heidegger moves through the sphere of life to that of personal existence, which he utilizes unremittingly for a religious purpose, but on the other hand he is also confined by this sphere" (*PSF* 4: 203). Cassirer then makes his own position even more clear by upholding " . . . the broader, more universal, *idealistic* meaning of religion and the idealistic meaning of history. In *it* we behold liberation and deliverance from the 'anxiety' which is the signature, the basic 'state-of-mind' of finite dasein."

Cassirer's biographers seem to agree that we find the main distinction between the two in Heidegger's *Endlichkeit* (how human knowledge is finite) and Cassirer's *Unendlichkeit* (belief in man's ability to transcend and expand his situation here and now, Meyer 2006: 169).[14] Although there was no hope of reaching a consensus across this divide—a conflict between two incompatible worlds, according to Ferrari (2003: 257)—willingness to explore central topics and to establish a common dialogue was nevertheless apparent on both sides.

This is where Michael Friedman (2000) picked up the thread in *A Parting of the Ways: Carnap, Cassirer, and Heidegger*. The willingness to explore central themes and the commitment to a common dialogue we have seen in Cassirer and Heidegger, despite the distance between the two, exemplifies what was a general tendency in the years up until the Nazis came to power. Friedman described it as an ongoing and constructive dialogue between the different schools of thought, with logical positivists on the one side and representatives of what was to become the continental school on the other, and Cassirer and his followers somewhere between. After the spring of 1929, historical circumstances—most of all, the rise of Hitler—led to the emigration of many outstanding intellectuals and the resulting divergence between the analytic Anglo-Saxon tradition and the continental European. The constructive dialogue ended. The result was two very different schools of thought, now practiced for the most part in isolation from one another.

4   The Parting of the Ways and the Divide in Organizational Theory

In this chapter, I discuss how the parting of the ways led to two very different schools of thought in organizational theory. As analytic philosophy gradually dominated the U.S. and England, continental European philosophy became dominated by the radical Heidegger. The first fueled the tradition within organization theory and management education that has been strongly criticized by Mintzberg (2004), Czarniawska (2003), Ghoshal (2005), and others. The latter has served as a major influence on the expansion of relativistic schools such as deconstruction, poststructuralism, and postmodernism. I discuss the division in organization theory and attempt to position Cassirer in relation to some of the most influential schools in the interpretive tradition of organizational theory.

TWO TRADITIONS

Simply stated, Ernst Cassirer was in a position between the positivists and the radical Heidegger, both as a mediator in the sense that he took part in and facilitated debates between the two philosophical positions, and as a philosopher who developed a non-dualistic theory. According to Friedman (2000), the ways parted after Cassirer left Germany, to the extent that the two traditions became estranged. This parting led to something that resembled mutual incomprehension, " . . . linguistically, geographically, and conceptually" (Friedman 2000: 157). Analytic or scientific philosophy gained dominance in the U.S. and England. Heidegger's radical philosophy came to dominate continental Europe.

If philosophy was detached from organization theory, it would not make much sense to write a book about the parting of the ways and management education. But that is, of course, not the case. The philosophy of science is an important basis of organizational theory (Scherer 2003). If a divide in philosophy occurs, we should at least expect to see traces of the split in organization theory as well. Anglo-Saxon organizational theory should now, as a general tendency, have a bias towards an ontology and epistemology that leans on analytic philosophy, whereas we should expect to find more relativistic, radical organizational theory on the European continent.

According to Fiol and O'Connor (2008), that is absolutely the case. A fascinating and dysfunctional divide exists between North American and European scholars (Fiol and O'Connor 2008: 251). Fiol and O'Connor pointed out the tremendous North American dominance that favors positive management research and used the Academy of Management (AOM) as an example: The AOM is, according to the academy's own Web site, the leading professional association for scholars in management and organization, as well as the oldest and largest scholarly management association in the world. By August 2008, it had 18,595 members from 104 nations. All the editors of their many journals were American, as were 12 of the 15 board members and 72 of the 79 AOM fellows. A list of journals developed by one of the AOM divisions in August 2008 did not include a single European journal. In an attempt to develop a European identity, and partially in opposition to the AOM and to the American tendency to favor positivist research, the European Group for Organizational Studies (EGOS) was founded in 1973, and the European Academy of Management (EURAM) was founded in 2000 " . . . explicitly to counter AoM's positivist perspective" (Fiol and O'Connor 2008: 252).

Fiol and O'Connor (2008) claim that the divide has become schizophrenic. However, they do not make a call for stronger integration in order to cure this schizophrenia. "The ultimate objective is for European and N. American (as well as other) research communities to feel strength in their distinctive identities in order to then, simultaneously, feel a bond of commitment to a common research cause" (Fiol and O'Connor 2008: 253).

What they long for—a commitment to a common research cause based on separate identities and mutual respect for different positions—sounds indeed very much like Friedman's (2000) portrayal of the 1920s, when a common ongoing interaction and dialogue occurred between positivistic and radical scholars.

A second portrayal of the divide in organizational theory was undertaken by Daved Barry and Hans Hansen (2008). They describe Europe as preferring research that is enjoyable, edifying, humorous, edgy, sublime, melancholic, and wistful, with an emotional and aesthetic appeal and a cultural depth that ought to converse with the Western social, philosophical, and literary traditions in order to be credible. However, they conclude, all this makes research utterly messy from the North American positivistic viewpoint.

Joanne Martin (2003) portrays a "continental divide":

> Much of the organizational literature, like most fields of social science, reads as if scholars could discover and accurately represent the objectively "true" nature of the empirical world, in accord with being-realism

and representational epistemology. This is the dominant view in the U.S., particularly in mainstream organizational journals. In contrast, European scholarship often remains open to other viewpoints. In accord with this emphasis on objectivity, in the United States most doctoral students are thought to do organizational research according to the scientific method, using deduction and induction to prove or falsify hypothesis.

(Martin 2003: 396)

Martin relates the split in organizational theory to underlying ontological and epistemological assumptions. On the one side of the divide, we find the "being-realism" and the "representational epistemology"; on the other side, we find the idea of a socially constructed world.

The two traditions differ significantly in methodology and the use of explanations. Jon Elster (1983) claimed that one may classify the sciences according to method, underlying interests, and modes of explanation. In natural sciences, hypothetic-deductive methods are valid as verification. However, when it comes to the use of the hermeneutic method in the arts and aesthetics and dialectic methods in the social sciences, it becomes difficult to tell if they are contributing to theory building or to verification.

Some of the difficulties in establishing a common cause become clear in the way Elster (1983) explained the differences, and which I have tried to illustrate in Figure 4.1.[1] The belief in and the use of very different modes of explanation challenge researchers to go beyond their traditions. For example, the meaning of the actor's intentions may be essential in the social sciences but highly questionable in biology and irrelevant in physics. Thus, one cannot apply functional explanations straightforwardly to social systems, according to Elster.[2]

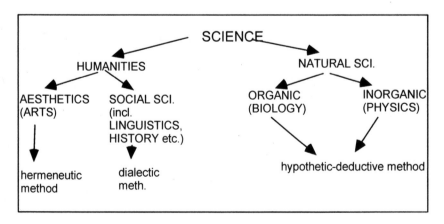

Figure 4.1 The use of methods in the natural sciences and the humanities.

FUNCTIONALISTIC AND INTERPRETIVE
THEORY AS COMPETING PERSPECTIVES

Elster (1983) pointed to differences that run deeply in the sciences. Martin (2003), Barry and Hansen (2008), and Fiol and O'Connor (2008) have shown us that these differences have divided organization theory and management education as well. A cut-down version of the dichotomy is illustrated in Table 4.1.

This crude simplification does not acknowledge many relational, processual, and non-dualistic theories. However, the dichotomies illustrate how the split in organization theory is often depicted. The analytic tradition is commonly portrayed as a rational approach with a focus on surface phenomena, concreteness, finalities and causality, formal plans, quantitative goals and objectives, hierarchical organizational structures, knowledge as truth and as "thing," change as planned and preprogrammed, and a conception of management as programming and control. The interpretive tradition is, however, seen as concentrating on deep-level phenomena; values; norms; interpretations; feelings; sense-making; mental images; knowledge as "process"; change as adaption, exploration, and learning; and management as dialogue and ongoing construction of (shared) realities.

Linda Putnam (1983) discussed the divide in organization theory under the labels *functionalistic and interpretive* perspectives. She described the functionalistic perspective as being in accordance with the analytic

Table 4.1 Dichotomies in Organizational Theory

Material	vs.	Ideal
Atomistic	vs.	Connectivist
Nomotetic	vs.	Hermeneutic
Structure	vs.	Agency
Society	vs.	Individual
Spectator	vs.	Participant
Positivist	vs.	Constructionist
Explanation	vs.	Understanding
Manifest content	vs.	Latent content
Subject	vs.	Object
Fact	vs.	Interpretation
Knowledge as object	vs.	Knowledge as process
System	vs.	Lebenswelt
Surface structure	vs.	Deep structure

tradition in philosophy and the interpretive perspective as being a part of the radical tradition.[3]

Within management and organizational theory, the split between functionalistic and interpretive perspectives is often described as a competition (Putnam 1983). Putnam depicted functionalistic theory as the dominant one, understood as a global category of a broad range of positivist schools.[4] The interpretive perspective is seen as a counterpart, with its focus on the subjective, intersubjective, and socially constructed meaning of the actors. The two perspectives are, according to Putnam, in a sort of "conceptual bondage" where the interpretive approach may be understood as a reaction against the dominant position of the functionalistic perspective in general, and the use of functionalistic theory for social phenomena in particular. This approach implies that the two perspectives share some common attributes yet at the same time are in opposition to each other. Functionalistic theory, on the one hand, views social phenomena as concrete, materialistic phenomena—as different kinds of social facts. Social life, norms, values, and roles become hard and accurate statistical facts. Social reality is something that exists separately from individuals. Interpretive theory, on the other hand, views reality as socially made through words, symbols, and behavior. Roles, norms, and values are man's ways of giving meaning to social actions. Organizations and organizational structures and phenomena that can be illustrated through, for example, organizational charts are seen as results of human interaction and are dynamic. Within a functionalistic paradigm, they tend to have their own existence, separate from the actors. In other words, ontology is one important demarcation line between the two positions.

Putnam's (1983) two broad categories, the interpretive and functionalistic paradigms, are to a large degree in accordance with Friedman's (2000) two antagonistic positions within philosophy. Of course, the dichotomy does not reflect the full range of paradigms or schools that should be recognized in a discussion of the state of the art within organizational theory.[5] However, the separation between interpretive and functionalistic traditions helps illustrate how the ways parted after Cassirer.

This illustration of more than 300 years is far too simplistic, and does not pay tribute to the many contributions that do not fall neatly into the dichotomies (e.g., Ernst Cassirer). However, as a pedagogical device it can be used to illustrate how the ways parted and the different consequences of the underlying assumptions. As such, it also illustrates that the differences between the two approaches became evident when modern science became a seal of enlightenment. Modern science entailed an increased belief in man's ability to differentiate between falsehood and truth and to choose his destiny through rationality and deduction. Like Kant, Cassirer was a critical proponent of enlightenment. On the one hand, Cassirer's philosophy is permeated by a quest for truth and clarity and the belief in man's ability to choose his own destiny. On the other hand, he admitted the limitations of

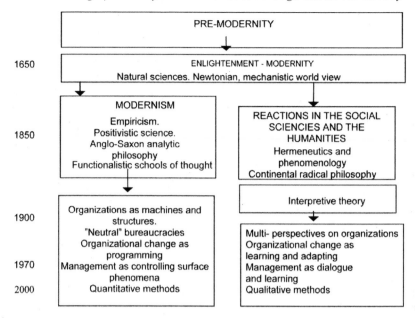

Figure 4.2 The two traditions.

the form of knowing that develops as a consequence of the rise of modern science. David Bidney (1949) explained:

> (. . .) Cassirer's attitude toward magic and myth is ambivalent and reflects the conflict between romantic and rationalistic traditions which he sought to reconcile. From an ethnological standpoint, he shares the view of the romanticists that myth constitutes an essential element in the evolution of human culture and thought. As a critical idealist, on the other hand, he is fundamentally a rationalist who participates in the struggle against the power of myth as an irrational, demonic force.
>
> (Bidney 1949: 529)

In his last book, *The Myth of the State* (1946), published one year after his death, Cassirer discussed how the Nazis used myths systematically in order to seduce a people. Cassirer realized that myths, which were traditionally described as the result of an unconscious activity and as a free product of imagination, had been made according to plan, artificially produced by "very skillful and cunning artisans" (Cassirer 1946: 282). Cassirer thus analyzed the rise of the political myth, returning to Malinowski's studies of primitive societies:

> This description of the role of magic and mythology in primitive society applies equally well to highly advanced stages of man's political

life. In desperate situations man will always have resource to desperate means—and our present-day political myths have been such desperate means. If reasons have failed us, there remains always the *ultima ratio*, the power of the miraculous and mysterious.

(Cassirer 1946: 279)

FROM SCIENCE WAR TO SILENCE?

Nearly 50 years after Cassirer's death, Kenneth Gergen (1992) reflected on the changes of the organizational context in a world of uncertainty and complexity. He described the historical phases from a romantic via a modernist to a postmodern conception and found parallels in all stages in organization theory. He found that the romantic dimension of organizational life was expressed through perspectives such as the Tavistock Institute's psychoanalytically based approaches, the human resource and human potential perspective (exemplified by Mayo, Mazlow, and McGregor), the Western emphasis on the bond between Japanese organizations and their members, the position stressing the personal resources essential for successful leadership (Fiedler), the position emphasizing organizational commitment, as well as the inquiries into the executive's appreciation of employees' needs for positive regard and the importance of empathy and dialogue (e.g., Cooperide and Srivastva).

Gergen (1992) believed that the romanticist influence of poets, novelists, philosophers, painters, composers, and architects contributed to the romantic dimensions of organizational life, especially regarding the notion of *the deep interior*. The truly significant aspect of the individual, " . . . that which rendered the persons uniquely identifiable as persons, is the existence of a repository of capacities or characteristics lying deeply within the human consciousness" (Gergen 1992: 209). To understand, express, and appreciate these capacities and characteristics requires a sophisticated introspective sensitivity and " . . . willingness to be wrenched from the contended perch of the ordinary" (209).

Gergen (1992) perceived the modernist world view as the counterpart of the romantic dimension, characterized by

(a) a revival of the Enlightenment beliefs of reason and observation,
(b) a search for fundamentals and essentials,
(c) a faith in progress and universal design, and
(d) an absorption in the machine metaphor (Gergen 1992: 211)

The functionalistic approach to social science described by Putnam (1983) is grounded on the same fundamental values, and both Putnam and Gergen understood functionalistic organizational theory as a consequence of modern ideas taken into organizations. The influence of modernity on organizational theory is strong. Gergen (1992) maintained that the rational laws of economic organizations and development evidently have served as the basis for scientific management, general systems theory including contemporary contingency theory (e.g., Lawrence and Losch), exchange theories (e.g., Homans), cybernetic theory, trait methodology (e.g., Fiedler), cognitive theory of individual behavior, and theories of industrial society (211–212).

Gergen (1992) described a world that lies waiting for the modernists to reveal its factuality through analysis. Its ontological status is relatively unproblematic. Our revelation of the hidden secrets of the world should take place through observation and reason, and should be reflected in language. The given world precedes language, which is merely a mirror or a slave where the universe is the master. This position has, according to Gergen, been challenged by hermeneutic (e.g., Husserl and Gadamer) and linguistic (e.g., Wittgenstein) philosophy, philosophers of science (e.g., Kuhn), critical theories (e.g., Habermas), ethnomethodology (e.g., Garfinkel), and feminist critiques (e.g., Calàs and Smirchic), as well as social constructionist and deconstructionist positions.

Postmodernism is often viewed as the sharpest opponent to modernism. It is depicted by Gergen as a blend of movements across disciplines that are suspect to the modernist view of language as a way of picturing the essentials of reality (Gergen 1992: 208). He claimed that the position is based on three related arguments:

First, *the real is replaced by the representational.* What we call "the real" is governed by the ideology of the caller, and attempts to inform society that "truths" or "realities" must be regarded with suspicion.

Second, *communal artifacts are seen as representations.* Language is placed in the hands of the community, Gergen held forth, in a relational space as a result of coordinated action. Language is more than a product of and from the individual mind to the surroundings. Language belongs to the community. Words remain nonsense as long as no other persons go along with their meaningfulness, and sense-making becomes a result of and an expression of collective manifestation or joint action.

Third, *ironic self-reflection is a characteristic of the postmodern position.* Self-reflection or critical suspicions of one's own suppositions is a prevailing theme in many sectors of postmodernism. The irony according to Gergen is a consequence of the paradox embedded in the removal of representation from reality as it is expressed in various propositions that are themselves representations. How can an argument negating the concept of truth itself be true? Gergen held forth that the central question remains unanswered in the sense that postmodernists, by their very position, make an answer within a postmodern paradigm impossible.

Gergen (1992) was a proponent of a postmodern turn in organizational theory. As a blend of movements across disciplines rather than a distinctive school, it was first and foremost defined by its critical stance against the modernist world view. The debate culminated in what has been regarded as a "science war." Thompson's (1993) claim that post-modernism had "reached the distant shores of organization theory" illustrates this antagonism. Pointing to the origins of postmodernism in architecture, art, and literature, he asked, "But what has a rejection of universal standards of beauty or a preference for pastiche got to do with organizations?" (Thompson 1993: 183). He concluded, " . . . the idea that it is nothing beneath the surface of representation is absurd and dangerous" (196).

Postmodernism took some serious blows, and the debate between real-ists and postmodernists declined. Thus, it may seem irrelevant or some-what outdated to discuss postmodernist organization theory in relation to Cassirer's philosophy. However, the end of the science war in organization theory in the 1990s does not imply that the positions were abandoned. When Fleetwood (2005) a few years ago described the status quo of orga-nization studies, he pointed to a recent cultural, linguistic, poststructural, or postmodern turn. Nevertheless, the common debate appears to have died down. Postmodernism in organizational theory seems to have been silenced, and its proponents have apparently found new and friendlier campfires around which to discuss their radical theories. If this is the case, it is surely a pity in light of Cassirer's intention for interparadig-matic dialogue.

Like interpretive theorists, Cassirer opposed positivism; but his solution was different from most radical interpretive schools'. In the following sec-tions, I will focus on three problematics related to interpretive theory: (1) interpretation and creation of meaning, (2) the role of language, and (3) the need for a critical stance. Thereafter I will attempt to position Cassirer in relation to these problematics.

INTERPRETATION AND CREATION OF MEANING

Several contributions have been made towards a postmodern theory of organizations. As one perhaps surprising example, Gergen (1992) referred to the works of Chris Argyris. Argyris and his associates made their rela-tionship to the hermeneutic tradition explicit (Argyris and Schön 1978), and defined their works as a contribution to what they called a *counter-view* of science. They underscored the need to view social phenomena as meaningful to human beings who enact them, in contrast to the main-stream account where the events of the natural world proceed independ-ently of subjective meaning. In the mainstream account, this difference does not make a difference for the logic of scientific inquiry, Argyris et al. held forth; but as proponents of the counterview they insisted that the difference is crucial (Argyris, Putnam, R., and McLain Smith 1985: 21).

Argyris et al. referred to Wilhelm Dilthey, who stressed the understanding of *meaning* and hermeneutic methods as the way of generating knowledge in the social sciences, and to the phenomenological tradition of Alfred Schutz that led to a new a understanding of the relation between science and community:

> Interpretations in the human sciences are second order, in the sense that they are built on (and presuppose some understanding of) the commonsense interpretations of social actors themselves. To be sure, there are procedural rules of scientific inquiry—for example, the methodological principles of sociology or anthropology. In this respect the social scientist is part of a community of inquiry, as emphasized in the mainstream account. What is distinctive to the human sciences, however, is that they must grasp the meanings embedded in another community of practice, that which they are studying.
>
> (Argyris et al. 1985: 21–22)

Here Argyris relates his work to what he calls a counterview tradition, and as such Gergen (1992) was right when he identified Argyris as a contributor to postmodern theory of organizations. However, here it is important to make a distinction between postmodern as a historical epoch and postmodernism as a theoretical position (Hassard 1996). Argyris is *postmodern* in the sense that he is an example of a tendency in a certain historical period, but he is not a representative of the radical, highly subjective, and often relativistic theoretical position of *postmodernism*. On the contrary, in all his works Argyris seemed to insist that there is a reality, also a social reality, that can be unveiled through thoughtful inquiry.

Argyris built on the ideas of action theories that are based on assumptions that often are hidden from the actors themselves. In a similar vein as Cassirer, Argyris talked about the gradual development of blindness as our perspectives become restricted. We not only construct our understanding of the world through learning processes; we also construct individual and collective defensive mechanisms that effectively hinder learning. Learning; then, is modification through reflective changes in one's theories about the world that leads to a more realistic and practical view of reality. This is an understanding of learning in the tradition of the humanities that " . . . may be said to be built on an epistemology of practical knowledge," Argyris argued (Argyris et al. 1985: 22).

The case of Argyris illustrates that neither an individual nor a social constructivist theory of learning has to lead to relativism, even if it shares many of the traits of radical postmodernism, such as the reluctance towards mainstream science and the importance placed on meaning. Argyris' methods also seem to have much in common with deconstruction and reconstruction, as recommended by Rosile and Boje (1996), but this does not turn him into a postmodernist.

Friedlander's (1989) "reconstructive learning" may be another illustration of the "softer" hermeneutic influence on learning theory that Argyris is a representative of: Reconstructive learning takes place in the tension between reality and what is desired. This discrepancy calls for a reconstruction of how we understand the world, a process where premises, intentions, and values are investigated. Reconstructive learning in this sense " . . . suggests the construction of new goals, policies, norms, styles rather than the simple modification of the old" (Friedlander 1989: 193). With Karl Weick (1979, 1982), the subjective and relativistic consequences of these construction and reconstruction processes become more emphasized: The individual takes an active role in creating new realities, a process where thinking and action are highly interwoven and reinforce each other. In organizations, managers typically face uncertain situations that involve gaps, discontinuities, and loose ties between people and events, and try to bridge these gaps when they cognitively tie the different elements together (Weick 1982). When resonance is established between action and some explanation, thinking intensifies action and action intensifies thinking. People enact and realize their ideas, and create their own realities. "The crucial phrase is 'real-izing [sic] their ideas.' By this I mean literally that people make real, or turn into reality, those ideas that they have in their heads" (287).

Organizations and organizational contexts also become ideas, created and then rediscovered by people, and these ideas become the basis for further actions. This approach implies that it becomes difficult to make clear distinctions between an organization and its environment. Organizations invest meaning in their environment and modify this meaning over time. "Thus, much of the talk about environments faced by organizations suffers from misplaced concreteness. As a result, boundaries are drawn between the supposed 'environment' and the supposedly corresponding 'organization' with more certainty than seems warranted" (Weick 1982: 273).

The theory of enacted sense-making is also discussed by Morgan (1986, 1991). Organizations become social models or metaphors constructed by the organizational actors. "Viewed in terms of these metaphors, organizational realities are to be seen as ongoing social constructions, emerging from the skillful accomplishments through which organizational members impose themselves upon the world to create meaningful and sensible structures" (Morgan 1991: 93).

The theory of enacted sense-making seems to imply that organizational members do not relate to an outside environment as such, but to interpretations of representations they themselves have created. The environment is located in the actors' brains, created as a result of their experiences, in order to make those experiences more meaningful. Weick (1982) concluded, "It seldom dawns on organizational theorists to look for environments inside of heads rather than outside of them" (274).

THE ROLE OF LANGUAGE

Whereas Argyris, Friedlander, Morgan, and Weick stressed the organizational members' active role in creating their own contexts, other interpretive scholars focused on the linguistic aspect of organizations. According to Morgan (1991), the notion of *language game* is a central metaphor in interpretive theory (92). The language game metaphor treats organizational realities as rule-governed symbolic structures that emerge when people engage in their worlds through the use of codes and practices in order to vest their contexts with meaningful form. Organizational realities exist in different uses of verbal and nonverbal language. Language is not merely a communicational or descriptive device; it is also ontological. Organizations are created and maintained as patterns of social activities through the use of language. To be a manager thus implies a sort of "being in the world" defined by language games in which a person must participate in order to be perceived as a manager as well as to act like one.

Pondy (1978) was one of the representatives of the language game metaphor in organization theory, building on Wittgenstein's notion that speaking a language is a part of an activity and a form of life in itself. The numerous language games can be at the same time different from each other yet partially overlap. Words constitute meaning as they are being used. Thus, the meanings of words change with the context, a process of shifting meanings that Wittgenstein called language games.

Pondy (1978) viewed leadership as a collection of games with some similarities, but without common characteristics that apply to all of them. As with grammar (defined as the relationship between sound and meaning), leadership also has a surface structure and a deep structure. But the deep structure of leadership has, according to Pondy (1978), somehow disappeared, and we are left with numerous theories of management, effectiveness, and leadership styles on a level that corresponds with grammar's surface structure. They are to a large extent observable and scientifically testable, according to natural scientific ideals. But the deep structures, and in particular meaning, have been neglected because of leadership's lack of a concrete observable existence. To understand leadership as language games implies a need for mapping " . . . the philosophical underpinnings of the role of meaning in leadership and behavior," according to Pondy (1978), who concluded, "At least it has had a profound influence on my own thinking about how meanings are established and what it means to communicate" (97).

THE NEED FOR A CRITICAL STANCE

Interpretive theory has a preference for the actor's point of view and seeks to understand the subjective meaning of people's *Lebenswelts*. However, one weakness in unilaterally taking the actor's perspective is that it tends to limit analysis at the manifest level to what is already within people's consciousness. This limitation causes problems if mechanisms and relationships influence people's behavior and the actors themselves are not aware of this influence. Also, if people's preunderstandings and assumptions are false or incomplete, an interpretive analysis will simply imply a reproduction of the actors' illusions.

To avoid such a reproduction (which by its very nature contributes to the status quo), critical theorists claim that we must leave the actor's perspective and take the spectator's stance in order to unveil the mechanisms and relationships that are hidden from us. This does not imply turning away from the actor and taking a distant macro perspective, but rather combining the actor's and the onlooker's perspectives. Both the subjective and the objective levels of social life are taken into account. Whereas interpretive approaches traditionally tend to be occupied with subjectivity, critical theorists maintain that social life will always be a result of conscious and intentional actions that lead to objective laws and structures that are hidden from the actors. Some of these objective phenomena may be aggregations of individual intentional actions that have created unintentional results. As such, they can be seen as anonymous forces that have their own objective existence.

From the critical theory perspective, the actors' subjective level is *Lebenswelt* (lifeworld), whereas *system* describes the objective level. The relationship between system and *Lebenswelt* and how free and valid communication can take place is the critical theorist's main interest, as in the example of Jürgen Habermas (1982). Whereas *communicative action* expresses the actions that take place as a result of the common understanding that constitutes man's *Lebenswelt, strategic action* characterizes man's individual and intentional actions within the world of system.

According to critical theory, the world of systems has somewhat colonized our lifeworlds. The influence of technical and economical experts on public discourse is one example of this colonization. Bureaucratization, management, and control through formalized administrative systems are examples from organizational life. It is in the critical theorist's interest to investigate the system mechanisms that hinder free and valid communication. As such, critical theory is not value-neutral in its approach. When analyzing organizational phenomena, the focus is more on the "why" than the "how." "The critical school views organizations as constructed realities, but it stresses the fact that this construction is not a free, voluntary process. ... Creation of meaning is not an arbitrary process that occurs through friendly negotiation and talk" (Deetz and Kersten 1983: 160). Critical theory applied to organizations is therefore concerned with the conditions that create and maintain the existing organizational reality, according to Deetz and Kersten.

Critical organizational theory stands out as an alternative that tries to steer clear of the dichotomy between functionalistic and interpretive schools

(Alvesson and Willmott 1992). Rooted in Marxism and German idealism and hermeneutics, it aims to investigate both the actor's subjective meaning and the unconscious structures and phenomena that often restrict the possibilities of a free and valid communication. Therefore, critical theory has the capacity to uncover the often concealed forces of the modernistic world of systems that seem to have a strong grip on today's organizations, without giving up on the ideas of rationality and liberation.

BETWEEN REALISM AND IDEALISM

Interpretive theory is a broad category, and the different schools treat central concepts such as interpretation, meaning, language, and the need for a critical stance differently. My task has not been to draw sharp distinctions between the schools, but rather to make use of them in order to determine the extent to which Cassirer would seem to agree or disagree.

When it comes to interpretation, most interpretive schools lead to an inevitable subjectivism, an individual relativity, as a result of how we construct our world, according to Margolis (1986). However, as I have already discussed, there are "soft" and "hard" versions of interpretive theory. The most radical schools claim that the real is replaced by the representational: the text is all there is, and thus talking about truth becomes meaningless. Language becomes essential in order to construct and make sense of the world. Cassirer seemed to agree that we construct our world, and that language plays an important role. However, identifying his closest allies within the interpretive tradition is far from obvious. Interestingly, Habermas (2001), also a defender of the ideas of enlightenment and the most prominent critical theorist of our time, praised Cassirer for having "opened up" the philosophy of consciousness by presenting language's world-disclosing capacity. Habermas also claimed that Cassirer had a stronger influence than Wittgenstein on the linguistic turn among German philosophers. However, this does not mean that Cassirer should be assigned the role of founder of radical constructivism, postmodernism, or poststructuralism. To which degree he influenced the linguistic turn is also highly questionable: Krois (2009) described how Cassirer undertook an important change when writing the second and third volumes of *The Philosophy of Symbolic Forms*. The first volume (1923) was named *Die Sprache* (Language), and placed him, according to Krois, in the same movement that was to be known as the linguistic turn. However; when he was in the midst of his writing, Cassirer broke out of the framework of philosophy of language and did a *symbolic turn*. Instead of contributing to the linguistic turn in philosophy that was to become associated with the Vienna Circle and Wittgenstein, he did the symbolic turn that Krois regarded as even more fundamental and wide-ranging, and that few philosophers have yet to follow.[6]

Cassirer regarded language as more than conventions. Words emerged from man's experiences with nature; feelings and emotions lay the foundation for speech, which in turn was the basis for language (*PSF* 1: 149). Language is only one of many symbolic forms, according to Cassirer, who, during writing the first volume of *The Philosophy of Symbolic Forms* (*PSF1*; "*Language*"), underwent a change and left the framework of philosophy of language, which was to become known as the linguistic turn in philosophy, and instead began his "symbolic turn" (Krois 2009).

Understood as a symbolic form, language has a mediating role. It may be liberating and open up the richness of the world, but it may also conceal reality. Language may lead us to reality, Cassirer held forth, but it may, as the case is with all symbolic forms, also hide aspects of reality through its particular logics and level of refraction. A consequence of this view is that Cassirer subscribed to neither a realist nor a nominalist position (Gawronsky 1949; Hamburg 1949: 102). He instead stressed that the symbolic forms offer different channels to reality and to different aspects of reality. We may never gain more than fractional knowledge, but we may obtain more or less *realistic* knowledge through developing the capacity to employ different symbolic forms. Hence, Cassirer would disagree with a view that restricts our understanding to the level of language.[7]

When postmodernists claim that an interest in discovering the nature of things is both naïve and misleading (Gergen 1992), they are of course in conflict with Cassirer, whose project may be understood as an effort to find access to the "real world." However, Cassirer also strongly rejected the positivist approach, which he claimed was a channel to the surface structures of reality only.

Cassirer believed in the liberating power of man. He took a critical stance, regarding philosophy as critical investigation. But, in contrast with postmodernists, Cassirer was not characterized by ironic distance and self-reflection. He was closer to classic critical theorists. Cassirer tried to transform the project of modernity in accord with the limitations of the modern conception of rationality, according to Lofts (2000). Cassirer achieved critical distance through reason and observation, and the symbolic form of science offered him the most elaborative means of critical investigation. However, science also hides and creates a distance from reality. In order to transcend the limitations of science and language, Cassirer thus called for the use of other symbolic forms, such as the form of art, which is more "immediate" and may illuminate hidden layers so that we may gain a more objective and realistic view. Through the harmony of symbolic forms, man may liberate himself.

Cassirer did not subscribe to a "hard" and mimetic correspondence theory of truth, but to a "softer" approach. We are immediately dealing with experience rather than knowledge. Knowledge is a result of how we mediate experience. Even the most immediate experiences are mediated.

But at the same time, making sense of experience requires knowing that something *is*, that we already have some objective knowledge. Symbolic forms are an example of a shared knowledge that already *is* and that forms our experience. Somewhat of a constructivist, Cassirer was "passing from the idealistic to the realistic view," according to Swabey (1949: 127), and, I believe, into an iterative realistic-idealistic-realistic view. Cassirer offered a processual and relational theory that was constructive, idealistic, and realistic at the same time.

But the core concept of Cassirer's theory is the symbol, or, to be more exact, the symbolic function of knowledge creation. One could thus easily believe that the heritage of Cassirer in organizational studies was in the hand of the symbolist branch of interpretive organizational theory. However, although Strati mentions Cassirer in his article "Organizational Symbolism as a Social Construction: A Perspective from the Sociology of Knowledge" (1998), Cassirer's philosophy and the symbolist approach as represented by Strati are different in several ways. For example, Strati defined organizational symbolism as a qualitative approach (Strati 1998: 1379). Cassirer, moving between the two poles of positive and radical theory, would probably claim that quantitative and qualitative approaches mediate reality differently, and he would probably not favor one over the other in his account of symbolism.

Also, it seems to me that Cassirer's theory of knowledge differs from Strati's (1998). Strati (1998) stated, "Knowledge is mediated by the universe of symbols, and cultures are constituted by symbolic textures" (1386). He then discussed how humans produce symbols, and the value of meaning of the symbols as provided by the humans who apply them. Thus far, Strati seemed to be in line with Cassirer. But Strati seemed to miss Cassirer's main contribution—the historical and cultural products of man's symbolic activities, the symbolic forms. Strati (1998) instead discussed the meaning of symbols, the construction of symbols, and the symbolization processes in organizations where " . . . there is no symbolization that does not relate to some organizational practices . . ." (1387). That is indeed what defines a symbol, but Cassirer did not stop there. Symbolism is merely a necessary condition in order to develop a theory of mankind, a first step in a philosophy of plural but at the same time unifying forms of knowing. Symbolic knowledge characterizes the human intellect, but the symbolic form characterizes the level of consciousness of mankind.

When Strati (1998) stopped at the symbols, he also stopped at the individual as the level of analysis. He gave an account of how individual perception and the creation of meaning take place in individuals, but he did not bring in the symbolic forms as different forms of knowing. He lost Cassirer's philosophy of simultaneous pluralism (multiple forms of knowing) and unity (the harmony of forms as objective knowledge). Instead, he presented symbolism as another way of understanding organizations, as yet an *alternative* to the dominant theories of organizations. Although Strati (1998) claimed that symbolism was not meant to be a new paradigm in organizational theory (1398), I read an attempt to demarcate symbolism from other forms of knowing. I think Strati himself, concerned with the tendency to employ a cognitive paradigm in organizational symbolism, illustrated this clearly: "Perhaps this is due to the close attention that organizational symbolism has paid to the mind—the intention being to mark its radical break with the positivist tradition" (Strati 1998: 1394). Cassirer did not work towards a break with positivism, but he did point out how insufficient and partial positive science was. Instead of demarcation and widening the gap, he strived to keep the dialogue running in order to comprehend the complexity of the modern world through a combination of plural forms of knowing.

Thora Ilyn Bayer (2002) stated:

> Cassirer's critique of modernity rests on the breakdown of a common context that can support the quest for self-knowledge. The "crisis in man's knowledge of himself," as Cassirer calls it, is based on the modern fragmentation of knowledge, which is also a fragmentation of the human self.
>
> (Bayer 2002: 100)

Cassirer identified the symbolic forms as a common, unifying context. The merit of symbolism, according to Strati (1998), is that it shifts the focus of organizational analysis to a "pluri-disciplinary understanding" (1398), but Strati failed to bring in the role of culturally developed forms of knowing as unifying mediators of impressions:

> Organizational symbolism yields a form of organizational knowledge which is a metaphor for organizational understanding. It is not a tool for cultural engineering in organizational life or a new paradigm in organizational theory. The symbolic approach, in fact, does not provide organizational scholars and organizational theorists with clear imperatives in regard to the understanding and managing in organizations. Instead, the organizational symbolism approach problematizes the meaning and focus of organization theory.
>
> (Strati 1998: 1398)

It appears to me as if Strati contributed to the fragmentation of knowledge against which Cassirer warned. We are left with a pluralism that stems from a multitude of voices and interpretations. Organizational symbolism becomes *one* perspective that underscores the variety of consciousness, a metaphor that does not offer recommendations and unification.

Where should one begin when seeking to build on an organizational theory that is critical, symbolic, relational, and processual? Writing from a philosophical perspective and not as an organizational theorist, Heintz Paetzold (2002-2) discussed how a critical cultural philosophy may be developed. Today, Paetzold claimed, we do not have such a school of philosophy. He suggested starting with the Frankfurt school's critical philosophy and Cassirer's philosophy, and bringing in Bourdieu's theory of cultural fields. His rationale for bringing together Cassirer and critical theory is that they are related in their philosophical attitude (e.g., drawing heavily on Hegel) and methodological nature. Both have the liberation of man as a goal (cultural liberation for Cassirer, and social and political liberation for critical theorists); both call for a combination of cultural and empirical social sciences; and both emphasize the role of ethics, mythodology, and art in related manners. Paetzold (2002-2) wrote, "From the outset, it should be clear that both, the critical theorists as well as Cassirer, favor the outlook that art has to be placed within the dynamics of a broader cultural life" (64).

Paetzold (2002-2) also suggested bringing in Bourdieu's theory of cultural fields. "Then our understanding of symbolic forms becomes nurtured with ingredients of social action, political struggle and modes of social recognition" (73). Cassirer had depicted a struggle of authority and dominance between symbolic forms, but in *The Myth of the State* (1946) he clearly expressed how an "innocent" form like myth could be used as a political instrument to manipulate a whole people. The combination of critical theory, Bourdieu's theory of *habitus* and social capital, and Cassirer's philosophy seem to me to be a good starting point for the development of an organizational theory based on symbolic forms.

ON THE PARTING OF THE WAYS IN ORGANIZATIONAL THEORY

I began this chapter with Michael Friedman's depiction of how the ways parted after Cassirer; illustrated how Martin, Barry and Hansen, and Fiol and O'Connor confirmed that the divide also was present in organization theory; and followed Linda Putnam's distinction between a functionalistic approach, understood as a concentrated manifestation of the modernist world view, and an interpretive approach to social science in general and organization theory in particular. I also identified some of the traces of interpretive or constructionist development towards radical and postmodern theories of organizations, in order to locate Cassirer in the interpretive landscape. Doing so was not an easy task.

As now should be clear, the interpretive approaches seem to have developed as reactions to the strong dominance of the natural sciences. Ernst von Glaserfeld (1984) described radical constructivism as a resistance movement and pointed to Vico (1668–1744) as the first true constructivist. Among the most prominent members of the resistance movement were also Schleiermacher (1768–1834), Dilthey (1833–1911), Husserl (1859–1938), Heidegger (1889–1976), Piaget (1896–1980), and Gadamer (1900–2002).

They differed in many respects, but all agreed that interpretation is required to create meaning; man constructs his world (cognitively or/and socially), and the result is a subjective world and a need for a suspicious attitude towards claims of objectivity.

Schools that heavily emphasize man as an interpreter and constructor of realities inevitably lead to an actor-oriented perspective. Taken into the study of organizations and the education of managers, this heavy actor orientation as a heritage from early hermeneutics and phenomenology has been criticized by critical scholars for being myopic and for losing the capacity to analyze the latent and unconscious objective levels of organizational realities. As a consequence, management research may contribute to maintaining the status quo in the context that has been studied.

Some interpretive schools may also contribute to the status quo through their particular understanding of the role of language. This linguistic turn in philosophy has fueled radical constructivist and postmodernist schools that build on the idea that the text is all there is. Thus, they may become rather uninteresting for the manager or the student of organization who is motivated to improve the "real world," not merely to scratch its surface structures. According to Gergen (1992), postmodern theories are replacing the real with the representational. As long as the "real" is governed by the ideology of the caller, claims of representing the truth must be regarded with suspicion:

> A genuine interest in discovering the nature of things in themselves seems both naïve and misleading. In this context, all the modernist attempts to determine through empirical investigation—through sensitive measuring devices, experimental variations and sophisticated statistical procedures—the actual nature of organizations become suspect.
>
> (Gergen 1992: 213)

That an interest in discovering reality is both naïve and misleading is a stance that Cassirer strongly would argue against. It is also a position that I have experienced as extremely difficult when I educate managers—especially practicing managers in executive programs. The problematics are not limited to radical antirealist positions that claim that the surface is all that is; they also involve theories that on the one hand accept the existence of a world "behind the text," but on the other hand deny access to reality. Von Glaserfeld (1995), a central name in radical constructivism, obviously felt a need to get things straight late in his academic career when he wrote, "I have never denied an absolute reality, I only claim, as the skeptics do, that we have no way of knowing it" (7).

Detachment from practice, and pessimism and cynicism toward the possibility of gaining knowledge of the "real" world and not only its surface structures, often lead my students to express a feeling of pointlessness and a waste of time. They do not expect to be offered a rhetoric of multiplicity, interpretation, construction, deconstruction, representation, fragmentation, indeterminacy, and skepticism when they are motivated to make a real difference in their own organizations. Probably due to my own background as a manager and organizational developer, I often find myself baffled by the postmodernists' ironic distance from their own role as scholars and from the possibility of developing applied organizational knowledge. The postmodern tendency toward cynicism, indifference, distrust, self-centeredness, irony, and distance comes dangerously close to resulting in a relativistic detached position of "anything goes because nothing works." Postmodernist theorists ironically point to modernistic approaches to administration, management, and development and change that are used—admittedly, often in vain—to explain, predict, and change organizational behavior. However, these normative approaches, despite all their shortcomings, "lure" managers to act and help them legitimatize their actions—and even more important, they may help managers unveil a reality that radical postmodernists deny themselves access to.

The divide in organization theory has consequences for the relationship between organization theorists and practitioners (Rynes, Bartunek, and Daft 2001). A postmodern school that primarily analyzes organizations from the outside, from an ironic distance, and in retrospect will be of little help to organizational practitioners. It will consequently leave the organizational domain to the modernists with their often oversimplified and mechanistic solutions. If interpretive, critical, or postmodern theories of organizations are to become alternatives to the modernistic approaches that seem to influence heavily the way we understand and manage today's organizations, these theories must be taken into living organizations to be used to understand organizational phenomena from within as well as to reduce, or at least to cope with, organizational uncertainty. Doing so calls for a stronger weight on normativity and implementation validity, in the sense that the theories need to become theories of action and not distant (and sometimes ironic) analyzing devices.

One may argue that the discussion between postmodernists and realists is history, a battle fought in the science war that occurred in the 1990s, and that I am wasting energy on an issue that is more or less settled. In my opinion, such a conclusion is superficial. The debates seemed to be more about the validity of science than about education (e.g., the education of managers). Having read hundreds or even thousands of student papers and exams over the last twenty years in the social sciences, I have noticed a "silent" turn in the direction toward the use of a constructivist jargon. I call this development "silent" for two reasons. First, in my academic communities we seldom comment on or discuss this turn. Second, the student's use of constructivist jargon has become nearly ritualistic. It has become increasingly common to place oneself as a social constructivist, without discussing the theoretical, methodological, and analytical consequences of taking this position. I suppose this trend mirrors reality in both the textbooks that are assigned and the way the curricula have been operationalized into teaching and learning processes.

It seems to me that the science war has ended, but at the same time that the distance between the positions has grown stronger. We have management education that seems to take for granted the realist and positivist assumptions of the world, as is reflected in Mintzberg's (2004) critique of MBA programs; but at the same time, a growing number of students position themselves as social constructivists, also in a more or less taken-for-granted manner. The consequence seems to be a split that is built on ontological and epistemological assumptions that are seldom brought up or critically challenged either within or between the positions.

Barry and Hansen's (2008) introduction to *The Sage Handbook of New Approaches in Management and Organization* clearly illustrates a growing frustration in parts of the organizational theory community. The battle lines became sharply drawn in the 1980s, with a polarization between positivism and postpositivism, or modernists and postmodernists. In the 1990s, the demarcation was reinforced by scholars defending and retaining incommensurability between the camps rooted in the 1960s polarization between functional and interpretive approaches. Barry and Hansen called for coming together "in the same building for the first time in a long time." They suggested that the time has come for the "relational," for a recombination of what has been fragmented, after years of fragmentation and pluralism. A relational turn will contribute to improved organizations, "so our arguments might now be healthier—more about how to make a great new place to work rather than drawing uncrossable lines on the floor" (Barry and Hansen 2008: 3).

5   Cassirer in the Light of Neuroscience

In this chapter, I discuss Cassirer's claims in light of the last two decades' research in neurobiology. I describe how neuroscience has shown that logical interpretation—cognition, rational thinking—takes place against a background of emotions. As such, it is initially an aesthetic experience. Sensing and cognition are interrelated, but sensing is "deeper" than cognition and closer to the immediate reality. I build particularly on Antonio Damasio's studies to show parallels and differences between Cassirer's theories and neuroscience. I close the chapter by concluding that becoming a two-eyed practitioner can be learned, and thus should be a part of management education.

A PHILOSOPHY OF HOPE AND LIBERATING POWER

We have already been presented Michael Friedman's depiction of how continental Europe was left for Heidegger to dominate after Cassirer was forced to leave Germany, and how what we call the continental tradition took its starting point from Heidegger (Friedman 2000). Heidegger versus Cassirer is in other words an important dividing line. Before we enter the realm of neuroscience, let me therefore recapitulate how Cassirer and Heidegger differ.

According to Hoel (2006), both Cassirer and Heidegger took Kant as a point of departure,[1] but they interpreted him differently. Heidegger's interpretation put weight on Kant's notion of the existence of two roots in man's epistemological development: *Sinnlichkeit* (sensibility) and *Verstand* (understanding). He claimed that these two stems had a common origin. Heidegger believed that this formerly unidentified root was Einbildungskraft, man's productive imagination. Because Einbildungskraft is temporal, it follows that man's existence (Dasein), as well as human knowledge, is finite. We are thrown into a world that we cannot escape. We do not have access to any forms of universal truths. For Heidegger, thought has no access to objectivity, language becomes just a social phenomenon, and his philosophy does not have access to transpersonal meaning, as Cassirer puts it (PSF 4: 202).

Following Heidegger's philosophy, this is, in essence, man's destiny. In contrast, Cassirer was not ready to renounce the Kantian view of man's capacity to choose his own destiny and to gain access to truth and objective knowledge. Cassirer viewed Kant's philosophy of Einbildungskraft as an opportunity to expand, redefine, and thus transform the idea of rationality that is manifested in symbolic forms. With the use of symbolic forms, man constructs a shared and objective reality that goes beyond the particular situation here and now. By transcending our practical existence, we may gain new insight and become truly free (Hoel 2006). Therefore, Cassirer's philosophy is a more optimistic philosophy of hope and liberating power.

Cassirer nevertheless refused to join forces with the positivists, who he believed were incapable of expressing and exhausting the truly positive aspects of psychology through their positive theory of knowledge (*PSF* 3: 27). Their strong belief in experience as the only source of knowledge and their emphasis on logical analysis as the favored way of clarifying philosophical problems were not in accordance with Cassirer's position.

Turning to examples from studies of brain injury patients, Cassirer illustrated how some patients lose the ability to think in general concepts or categories. When they lose their grip on universals, they become glued to the immediate facts and to concrete situations. The capacity to reflect is lost. Accordingly, these patients lose what Cassirer saw as a crucial ability to differentiate between the "real" and the "possible." In this sense, they are just like animals—or just like positivists, one might say: According to Cassirer, empiricists and positivists have always claimed that the primary mission of human knowledge is to give us the facts and nothing but the facts. But Cassirer believed that human knowledge by nature is symbolic knowledge. Thus, *meaning* becomes crucial because a symbol has no concrete existence as a part of the physical world. Instead, symbols have meanings. Through his philosophy of symbolic forms such as language, art, myth, religion, science, and history, he attempted to show how these forms mold our fluid sensory impressions so that they become clear and take form. This is a formative process by which the symbolic forms act as configurations towards being, and we do not end up with copies of an existing reality but to a unified and more realistic view (*PSF* 1: 107). Although he perceived his philosophy as an effort to unveil the ultimate reality and being itself, Cassirer made it clear that we are not to understand it as an attempt to establish an absolute correspondence between thought and reality. Thought does more than just express being. Instead, thought and reality "must permeate each other"; they must be seen as one instead of as separate elements (*PSF* 3: 2).

As we illustrated in Chapter 2, Cassirer described our experience with the world as a process from intuitive and immediate sensory impressions to a representation within the realm of language. The world is given to us through immediate sensations (*PSF* 3: 129). In *The Philosophy of Symbolic Forms,* he presented his philosophy in a broad, multifaceted, and scholarly way. In *An Essay on Man,* while still writing in a scholarly manner, he made his message more accessible to his new American audience by polishing his main points; elaborating on some of them; and adding chapters on myth, language, and science. In his discussion of how man experiences the world through a process from sensation to representation, he dwelled, as we saw in Chapter 3, on two specific symbolic forms, art and science (and to some degree art versus science and language). He claimed that art and science represent two different but complementary channels to reality, in contrast with each other but not in conflict or contradiction. However, a habitual blindness may gradually develop and conceal layers of reality, and we may end up using "just one eye." Thus, he called for a combined view, a way of understanding the world that draws on the two different ways of discovering reality.

Writing *The Philosophy of Symbolic Forms* in the 1920s and *An Essay on Man* in the 1940s, Cassirer drew on a number of examples from sensory studies and brain injuries of his own time, decades before new scanning techniques opened the brain for direct mapping. Because Cassirer based so many of his claims on what today might seem like sheer speculation, an intriguing question is to what degree the last decades' new insight into human consciousness has been able to prove or disprove Cassirer's theories.

In particular, two aspects guide my reading of neurobiology's research on human consciousness. First is the relationship that Cassirer describes between intuitive, immediate sensation and knowledge based on language, categories, and classification (i.e., the process from immediate sensory impressions to a representation within the realm of language and science). Second is Cassirer's claim that art is a channel to reality that intensifies and unites.

My aim is not to cast light upon the psychological aspects of sense-making. The individual is not my primary level of interest, nor are sensation and cognition my units of analysis. My intention is instead to take Cassirer into organizational theory and management education. So when I now turn to neuroscience, I do so merely to explore and, if possible, make Cassirer's ideas more actionable in organizational studies.

COGNITIVE SENSATION OR SENSITIVE COGNITION?

The famous Norwegian explorer, diplomat, and scientist Fridtjof Nansen (1861–1930) once said that a truth that is discovered with one's own eyes, although incomplete, is worth ten times a truth that one receives from others, because in addition to expanding one's knowledge, it increases one's ability to see. I would rephrase Nansen slightly: a truth that is discovered with one's body is worth ten times more than a truth that one discovers through reasoning, because in addition to expanding one's knowledge, it increases one's ability to feel.

Before turning to the few last decades' research on neuroscience, I want to share with the reader the experience that led me to this conclusion.

The CN Tower in Toronto, with a height of 553.33 meters, used to be the world's tallest building. At 342 meters, I enter the outdoor observation deck. I am nervous, but still I am able to enjoy the tremendous view. My wife takes photographs of me. We walk along the deck and enter the glass floor room. There, I suddenly become cold as ice.

In front of me is a glass floor, and beneath the floor is nothing but 342 meters of thin air. Worst of all, there are people walking on the floor of glass. A teenager is jumping up and down, as if he is trying to test the construction. A middle-aged overweight man stands on the edge of the floor for a couple of seconds before entering it. It just does not seem right. I can see the big man looking nervously at something that seems to be miniature cars beneath the 24-square-meter glass floor. I feel sick. Then my wife steps onto the floor and asks me to take her picture. My hands are trembling. I stand with my back against the wall in an attempt to feel safer. She asks me to join her on the floor. I am trying to move, but I am frozen. I tell myself to be rational. I remind myself that no accidents have occurred since the tower was built. I know, I know! And I remind myself what I have read somewhere: the floor is "strong enough to support at least a dozen hippos."

But thinking rationally is useless. Mere factual knowledge makes no difference. My feet will not move. Something is holding me back that is much stronger than my rational brain.

I learned from trembling in the tower that emotions are strong drivers. This is something I *thought* I already knew, but I had to admit that I did not *really* realize it until I experienced it bodily. Even though I so many times have asked my children to think rationally when they are scared of something, my attempts at rationally convincing myself to enter the glass floor were useless. I knew, rationally, that it was perfectly safe. But I was scared, and my body refused to move. At least, that is how it felt. My brain could not convince my body. On the way down from the tower, I found a leaflet that described how amazingly strong the glass floor is. It can actually withstand a pressure of 4.1 Mpa. One Pascal (Pa) is, according to Wikipedia, $\equiv 1$ N·m^{-2} $\equiv 1$ J·m^{-3} $\equiv 1$ kg·m^{-1}·s^{-2}. I guess hundreds of overweight middle-aged men could have walked on that platform—and maybe a hippo as well. I started to become convinced, and I decided that the next time I am in Toronto, I will definitely walk on the glass floor. So I really do think that facts and rational thinking may have a say after all, even in a case like mine. However, I recently read that the glass is just 6.4 cm thick. *6.4 cm thick!* That isn't much! Can you feel it? If not, just think about it: 6.4 cm is actually *very thin*, especially taking into consideration that it is 342 meters above the asphalt! Well, Wikipedia informs me that some people experience acrophobia in the CN tower, defined as an extreme or irrational fear of heights.

One could believe that an insight into the brain, the center of thinking and rationality, implies a reinforcement of the belief in man as a rational being, steered by an organic version of a fast, powerful computer called the brain. If we turn to recent research of the brain, we see that this does not seem to be the case. On the contrary, it seems that new insights have blurred and to some degree removed the borders between thinking and sensation, rationality and emotions, and body and mind.

New methods of studying the human brain have paved the way for new knowledge of man's relating to the world, as well as to a confirmation of earlier conjectures. More than a decade ago, neurologists such as Joseph LeDoux (1996) and Antonio Damasio (1994) offered new insights into the role of emotions in the workings of our brains. They studied people with brain damage, conducted structured scientific experiments, and scrutinized the human brain with the help of new scanning technologies. Soon the importance of the body and emotions became evident. In his *Descartes' Error* (1994), Damasio indicated the need for a paradigm shift away from a separation of cognition and emotions, and away from a view where emotions more or less equal irrationality. In the brain, emotions originate from the reptilian brain or limbic system, manifesting themselves as autonomic responses over which the conscious mind has little control. When an observation is being interpreted, it is only half interpreted by the time it reaches the limbic system. However, by that time, emotional memory is already part of the process of interpretation and may cause the limbic system to react before any rational interpretation has taken place. That is, as a result of the limbic system's autonomic reaction, emotion causes our attention to shift towards the stimuli that has caused that emotion (du Plessis 2005). Logical interpretation (e.g., cognition and rational thinking) thus takes place against a background of emotions. The feeling associated with the situation that caused the emotion, called the *soma,* becomes a memory of how the body felt when the observation happened. Contradicting Descartes, one could thus say that the absence of emotions does not secure a rational process, but hinders it. Emotions may actually pave the way for wise decisions.

Neurologists of the early 1990s found that emotions are physiological reactions that occur autonomously in the limbic system as part of the interpretation of observations. These reactions take place prior to the interpreted observation being used in the rational frontal lobes. An emotion has two dimensions, *direction* and *intensity.* The direction of the emotion may signal whether we should get closer or further away from the confronting situation. The intensity (or urgency) tells us how strongly and how quickly we should react to the stimuli. It follows that emotions and rationality should not be regarded as conflicting processes, but rather as processes working together for the best result. One role of emotions is to set the soma against which observation is rationally interpreted. By doing so, emotions direct attention, helping us to steer clear of or to approach situations and things. This viewpoint is known as the *somatic marker hypothesis* (Bechara and Damasio 2005; Dalgleish 2004; Damasio, Everitt, and Bishop 1996).[2]

Emotions help us sort different possibilities, a function that we often associate with rational thinking. When emotions are removed, decision-making may become more difficult. We then lack the structuring and directing element that emotions offer. Because emotions play a role before rational thinking starts, they aid our decision-making process. Emotions are "deeper" in the epistemological process than conscious thinking is.

In *Blink: The Power of Thinking Without Thinking* (2005), science journalist Malcolm Gladwell described an experiment conducted by a group of University of Iowa scientists. It was a simple gambling game. In front of the subject were four decks of cards. Two of them were blue, and two were red. Each card in those decks either won or lost the subject a sum of money. The subject was asked to turn cards from any of the two decks, in order to maximize the winnings. The scientists had, however, not told the subjects that the red decks were a minefield. They might win, but when they lost on the red cards they lost substantially. The only way to win was by taking cards from the blue decks. Then the subject won small sums steadily and at the same time risked small penalties. What the experiment showed was essentially that the gamblers figured out the game before they realized it. They also began making adjustments in their gambling strategy before they were consciously aware of those adjustments.

The scientists measured the activity of the sweat glands below the skin in the palm of the gamblers' hands. They found that the players started generating stress responses to the red decks by the tenth card. But it took forty more cards before they were able to say that they had a hunch about what was wrong with the decks. Even more impressive was the fact that the scientists proved that the gamblers changed their behavior, in the sense that they started favoring the blue cards.[3]

Gladwell used the Iowa experiment to illustrate that our brain employs two different strategies to make sense of a situation. The first is quick and intuitive, whereas the second is conscious and rational. Even though we do not know why we prefer the blue decks, we are pretty sure that they are the best, and we adjust our strategy. That happened to the test persons after fifty cards. But it took eighty cards before they came up with a logical explanation; a theory; or a conscious, logical, and definite strategy. The drawback of the first strategy is that it operates, at least at first, below the surface of consciousness, sending messages through indirect channels such as the sweat glands in the palms of our hands.

EMOTIONS AS MEANS FOR THE BRAIN

Antonio Damasio was one of the researchers who conducted the Iowa card game experiment described by Malcolm Gladwell (Damasio 1994: 212–222). He has since become one of the most prominent of the neuroscientists who surfaced in the early 1990s. After publishing *Descartes' Error* in 1994, he wrote *Looking for Spinoza* (Damasio 2003), based on his knowledge from researching the human brain in an investigation of philosophical issues and

Spinoza in particular. In an attempt to reach a conclusion, or what he called a path towards the happy ending, he called for " . . . a life of the spirit that seeks understanding with enthusiasm and some sort of discipline as a source of joy—where understanding is derived from scientific knowledge, aesthetic experience or both" (Damasio 2003: 283).

The elimination of emotion and feeling from the human picture entails an impoverishment, according to Damasio (2003).[4] If social emotions and feelings are not properly installed, and if the link between social situations and joy and sorrow breaks down, we are not able to categorize what we experience in our autobiographical memory in relation to the emotion/feeling mark that tells us what is "good" or "bad" (Damasio 2003: 159).

Damasio distinguished between emotions and feelings. We have background emotions, primary emotions, and social emotions. Background emotions are important, but not prominent in our behavior. They are revealed as "state of being" (e.g., good or bad). "When asked 'how we feel,' we consult this 'state of being' and answer accordingly" (Damasio 2003: 44). On a level above background emotions, we find such primary (basic) emotions as fear, anger, disgust, surprise, sadness, and happiness. Thereafter, Damasio placed the social emotions (e.g., sympathy, embarrassment, shame, guilt, pride, jealousy, envy, gratitude, admiration, indignation, and contempt).

"Emotions provide a natural means for the brain and mind to evaluate the environment within and around the organism, and respond accordingly and adaptively" (Damasio 2003: 54). In some cases, our apparatus of emotions evaluates "naturally," and our apparatus of conscious mind coevaluates. However, emotions evaluate whether our conscious mind coevaluates or not. We have, for example, been conditioned to feel uncomfortable in certain places, such as places where we have experienced fear as a child, but we do not know why.

Actually, few if any objects are emotionally neutral to us as grown-ups. They evoke emotional reactions, from strong to weak or barely perceptible. As we grow up, we learn to modulate the execution of emotions. We attempt to shape our natural responses to bring them in line with the requirements of the given culture. When an emotional response occurs without conscious knowledge of the emotional component stimulus, the emotion nevertheless reveals the result of our appraisal of the situation.

The small area in the middle of our brain, the amygdala, has been extensively researched in relationship to the triggering of emotions. The normal amygdala may actually trigger emotions whether we are aware of the presence of emotionally competent stimuli or not. Brain scans reveal that the amygdala has the ability to detect emotionally competent stimuli nonconsciously. That is, even if we are not aware of what we are sensing, the amygdala "picks it up." Damasio (2003) referred to the research of Arnie Ohman and Raymond Dolan, who found that we can learn, covertly, that one certain stimulus but not another (e.g., a particular angry face but not another angry face) is associated with an unpleasant event.

The emotionally competent stimuli (e.g., angry or happy faces) are detected very quickly, ahead of selective attention. Whether one is paying attention or not, Damasio (2003) concluded, emotionally competent stimuli can be detected; subsequently, attention and proper thought can be diverted to those stimuli.

FEELINGS AS MENTAL REPRESENTATIONS

The triggering and execution of an emotion leads to an emotional state. The continuation and intensity of this state is then dependent on the ongoing cognitive process. Thus, the emotion may be sustained or amplified. At this stage, emotions lead to *feelings*. "Curiously, by the time the process reaches the stage of assembling feeling, we are back in the mental realm—back in the flow of thoughts where, in normal circumstances, the entire emotional detour began" (Damasio 2003: 65).

So the emotion sadness comes before the feeling sadness. Emotions give rise to feelings. Feelings are cognitive representations of emotional states. Feelings affect our ongoing thinking and thus can alter future thinking, planning, and future behavior (Damasio 2001: 102). We have a "body-minded brain": mental processes are grounded in the brain's mapping of the body (Damasio 2003: 12). Emotions occur in "the theatre of our body," feelings in the "theatre of our mind."

Damasio claimed that science has shunned the study of feelings. Feelings have, as is the case with consciousness, been viewed as beyond the bounds of science. They are mysterious, private, and inaccessible. However, Damasio realized that the neurobiology of feelings is no less viable than the neurobiology of memory or vision. What he found was that evolution seems to have assembled the brain machinery of emotion and feeling in installments.

> First came the machinery for producing reactions to an object or event, directed at the object or at the circumstances—the machinery of emotion. Second came the machinery for producing a brain map and then a mental image, an idea, for the reactions and for the resulting state of the organism—the machinery of feeling.
>
> (Damasio 2003: 80)

The first level, emotional response, permits organisms to react effectively but not creatively to threatening events. The second level, feelings, presents us with a mental alert for good or bad circumstances. It also prolongs the impact of emotions by lastingly affecting attention and memory. Damasio claimed that this is an important condition for projection and coping with future challenges. "Eventually, in a fruitful combination with past memories, imagination, and reasoning, feelings led to the emergence of foresight and the possibility of creating novel, non-stereotypical responses" (Damasio 2003: 80).

Feelings are a mental representation of parts of the body or of the whole body as operating in a certain manner. A feeling, in its narrow sense of the word, is "the idea of the body being in a certain way" (Damasio 2003: 85). We may substitute "idea" for "thought" or "perception," according to Damasio. We are referring to a representation of a particular state of the body. Feelings are perceptions, and Damasio proposed that the most important support for their perception occurs in the brain's body maps, which refer to states as well as parts of the body. The perceptions of the body are accompanied by perceptions of thoughts. At this point, we have reached a higher level, in the sense that the perceptions of thoughts result from constructing metarepresentations of our own mental processes. One part of the mind represents another part of the mind. Thus, " . . . a feeling is the perception of a certain state of the body along with the perception of a certain mode of thinking and of thoughts with certain themes" (Damasio 2003: 86).

DESCARTES' ERROR

It should come as no surprise that Damasio (1994) addresses what he called Descartes' error, which was also the title of one of his books. His concern is both for what he calls "the dualist notion with which Descartes split the mind from the brain," as well as the modern versions that perceive the brain and mind as related, but only in ways where the mind is seen as " . . . a software program run in a piece of computer hardware called brain; or that brain and body are related, but only in the sense that the former cannot survive without the life support of the latter" (Damasio 1994: 248).

Damasio maintains that Descartes made several errors, but he singles out the renowned *Cogito ergo sum* ("I think, therefore I am"):

> Taken literally, the statement illustrates precisely the opposite of what I believe to be true about the origins of mind and about the relation between mind and body. It suggests that thinking, and awareness of thinking, are the real substrates of being. And since we know that Descartes imagined thinking as an activity quite separate from the body, it does celebrate the separation of mind, the "thinking thing" (*res cogitans*), from the nonthinking body, that which has extension and mechanical parts (*res extensa*).
>
> (Damasio 1994: 248)

Damasio describes the evolution of human consciousness as a historical development. Starting at some point in evolution as an elementary consciousness that resulted in "a simple mind," Damasio describes a development that led to greater complexity of the mind and the possibility of thinking. Even later came the use of language to organize communication and thinking:

> This is Descartes' error: the abyssal separation between body and mind, between the sizable, dimensional, mechanically operated, infinitely divisible body stuff, on the one hand, and the unsizable, undimensioned, un-pushpullable, nondivisible mind stuff; the suggestion that reasoning, and moral judgment, and the suffering that comes from physical pain or emotional upheaval might exist separately from the body. Specifically: the separation of the most refined operations of mind from the structure and operation of a biological organism.
>
> (Damasio 1994: 249–250)

From a neurobiological standpoint, Damasio trashes the whole idea of a disembodied mind. Not only does he blame the Cartesian view in the philosophy of science, but he also holds neuroscientists responsible for having reinforced this split through their neglect of emotions in their discussions of an integrated body and mind. His explanation is that emotions have been regarded as too subjective and indefinable for neuroscientific research and studies of the brain. Instead, focus has been directed towards that which appeared more objective and concrete. However, Damasio proposes that emotions are no more elusive than, for example, memory and perception; they are actually more concrete and objective. He blames post-Cartesian and neo-Kantian approaches for the neglect of emotions. Emotions came to be regarded as the very antithesis of one good thing called science. "And who would want to spend a lifetime to understand the very opposite of one good thing?" (Damasio 2001: 101).[5]

THE ROLE OF EMOTIONS IN THE ORGANIZING OF SOCIETIES

A result of the Cartesian split was the neglect of the role of feelings and emotions, and an understanding of thinking as an activity separate from the body. Intelligence belongs to the brain; emotions are not rational, and ought to be excluded or controlled by rational thinking.

The neglect of emotions has further consequences for social life, according to Damasio (2001). First, if emotions are left out, it becomes more difficult to understand the relationship between an organism and society and culture, which Damasio regards as one of the most complex aspects of an environment. Second, survival in complex environments becomes more difficult to study. Third, because emotions play a role in memory, neglecting emotions makes it difficult to understand memory, because they " . . . are so closely coupled that one cannot understand the latter without the former" (Damasio 2001: 102). Fourth, he addresses the role of emotions in reasoning and decision-making, and concludes that making sense of " . . . the mechanisms behind the finest human achievements—high reasons, ethics, law, and artistic, scientific, and technological creativity—cannot proceed without an understanding of emotion" (Damasio 2001: 102).

Essentially, Damasio (2003) claims that new insight from neuroscientific research has important consequences for social life and the social sciences, a claim that is mirrored in his interest in philosophy. Damasio was particularly interested in Spinoza because of Spinoza's claim that the mind and the body are parallel attributes of the same substance. This claim, Damasio pointed out, stood out in a sea of conformity at that time. "More intriguing, however, was his notion that the human mind is the idea of the human body" (Damasio 2003: 12). Damasio's own research led him to the conviction that mental processes are grounded in the brain's mapping of the human body, and that leaving out emotions and feelings deteriorates our scientific attempts to understand and improve human life. Consequently, he has become a spokesperson for the combination of the natural sciences and the humanities. "Science can be combined with the best of a humanist tradition to permit a new approach to human affairs and lead to human flourishing" (Damasio 2003: 283).

In Damasio's view, feelings and emotions are no more subtle than other biological phenomena that can be studied objectively (Damasio 1989). Despite the important role they play in the cognitive processes (e.g., decision-making, learning, and perception), they have gained little attention or have been seen as mysterious in science. Another consequence is that their importance to ethical behavior has been understudied. "The elimination of emotion and feeling from the human picture entails an impoverishment of the subsequent organization of experience" (Damasio 2003: 159).[6]

For us to succeed in categorizing the experiences of events in our autobiographical memory record, our social emotions and feelings must be properly deployed, and the relationship between social situations and joy and sorrow must not be broken down. Then the construction of such notions as "goodness" and "badness" will be prevented. In that case the result is a breakdown in the cultural construction of what ought to be, according to its good or bad outcomes.

According to Damasio (2003), the absence of emotions and subsequent feelings would preclude the development of cultural instruments. In that case, society would be without ethical behavior, religion, political organization, justice, or law; or these constructs would be detached from everyday living practice as a technical, intellectual structure. Damasio does not claim that neurobiology alone can explain ethical behavior or the lack of ethical behavior; he stresses that insights from fields such as law, religion, ethics, anthropology, sociology, psychoanalysis, and evolutionary psychology are needed as well. However, he points to the historical development of man's consciousness and claims that feelings must have been a necessary grounding for ethical behaviors long before humans began the deliberate construction of intelligent norms and conducts. He refers to the way animals as well behave in what seems to be an ethical manner. They may exhibit sympathy, attachment, humble submission, and dominant pride. For example, rhesus monkeys refrain from pulling a chain that would deliver food to them if pulling the chain also would cause another monkey to receive an electric shock. Some monkeys would not eat for days. The monkeys that had previously been shocked were most likely to behave altruistically (Damasio 2003).

Accordingly, ethical behavior is not an exclusively human trait; it does have forerunners. "But human ethical behavior has a degree of elaboration and complexity that makes it distinctively human" (Damasio 2003: 161). Underlying these complex and elaborated constructs, however, emotions and feelings play a pivotal role. They index the state of life in any human group, and are indispensable for intelligent reflection to take place. "Intelligent reflection on the relation between social phenomena and the experience of feelings of joy and sorrow seems indispensable for the perennial human activity of devising systems of justice and political organizations" (Damasio 2003: 165).

NEUROSCIENCE AND CASSIRER'S CALL
FOR AESTHETIC UNDERSTANDING

The main character in the Norwegian novelist Tarjei Vesaas' (1897–1970) book *The Birds* (2002; published in 1957 as *Fuglane* in Norwegian) is Mattis, a mentally retarded man in his late 30s. Mattis has invented a secret test, which he applies when he walks the dusty roads in his valley looking for work at the farms. When he comes to a crossroad, he stops and listens to his legs. "If you want to go in that direction, then you give me a signal," Mattis instructs his legs. If he does not feel any motion in his legs, he continues forward instead. The legs are wise, Mattis says. He ends up at the local store and buys candy. "No work today either," Mattis concludes.

A candidate for the Nobel Prize in Literature in 1964, 1968, and 1969, Vesaas was a novelist with a profound insight into human psychology. In *The Birds,* he depicted Mattis as a mentally retarded man with a childish, sensitive, imaginative, empathic mind and an inborn feel for poetry. Mattis is undoubtedly in connection with his emotions, but he does not possess the ability to attach his bodily emotional sensations with rational thinking. When Mattis' world turns more complex, he has no mental tools to handle the confusion. The moving story of Mattis then turns into a tragedy.

Damasio and the neuroscientists found that the brain is far from alone. The brain is body-related; it does not turn outward, isolated from the human body. The more the neurobiologist maps the brain, the more evident the importance of bodily sensations becomes. When something happens, we sense before the brain starts the important work of rational reasoning and classifications. The problem with Mattis is that he does not have the rational tools, the mental capacity, or the ability to think logically and arrive at useful inferences that can help him cope with complexity. His channel to the world is through his senses, but it more or less stops there. According to Damasio (2003), we make sense of the world when our mind makes sense of our body: we interpret bodily reactions, emotions, and feelings. Here Damasio and Cassirer seem to be joining forces: like Damasio, Cassirer believed that the world is given to us through immediate sensations. What neuroscience does not do is to bring in symbolic forms as different forms of knowing. Sensation precedes thinking, but through symbolic forms we allocate particular qualities to and mold our sense impressions. Cassirer claimed that, perhaps contrary to the common view, art is a path to an objective view of the world. Through art we discover the external world, and we do so in a different way than through science. Whereas science's path to the objective world is through the classification of our sense perceptions and as such leads to a simplified world, art's path is through illumination, intensification, and concentration. The tendency to approach the world unilaterally through science and language implies a gradual development of habitual blindness, according to Cassirer. In that case, it is necessary to develop the ability to "see with the eye of art." But we need both eyes to navigate in three-dimensional space. The unilateral use of any form of knowledge, including art, gradually leads to blindness.

The question then is *how* art illuminates, and how aesthetic understanding works. According to Cassirer, it takes place through a process from passive receptivity and through a symbolic function where our consciousness is differentiated and reality is formed. Symbolic forms (e.g., language, science, myth, and art) configurate and form our interpretations (*PSF* 1: 107). However, art configurates our understanding differently than the other forms do.

New scanning techniques of the human brain, such as positron emission tomography (PET), magnetic resonance imaging (MRI), and functional MRI (fMRI), may help us gain insight into some of these processes, including the role of art as illumination. A number of findings are depicted in Matthews and McQuain's *The Bard on the Brain: Understanding the Mind Through the Art of Shakespeare and the Science of Brain Imaging* (2003). In several ways, this book is parallel to Damasio's *Looking for Spinoza* (2003). The most obvious parallel is the attempt to bridge neuroscience and the humanities. Paul Matthews is a professor of neurology at Oxford specializing in brain imaging, and Jeffrey McQuain is a scholar of literature specializing in Shakespeare and Chaucer. As with the case of Damasio's book, the most convincing parts are the results of neuroscientific research. Matthews and McQuain's illustrations of which parts of the brain become active when we are presented new sense impressions (e.g., new words, smells, and colors) are, literally speaking, shedding light on the functions of the brain and the potential role of art. Shakespeare constructed more than 1,500 new words, according to Matthews. Brain scans tell us that novel words have a different effect on the brain than recurring words do. The more we use a certain word, the less our brain reacts. New words cause small "explosions" in our brain.[7]

Scanning techniques may to some degree help us see how art illuminates inward, inside the brain. Cassirer described how art also may illuminate outwards, the reality around us, and both Damasio and Cassirer depicted how this process goes both ways. Cassirer explained the role of the symbolic forms in this process, and how all forms in their particular ways may open as well as hide reality. They offer different directions and logics that lead to different aspects and layers of reality and subsequent understandings (*PSF* 3: 1). Art's particular contribution must be understood in terms of the logic of the humanities as to concentrate attention on and illuminate and intensify the deeper levels, whereas the quest for rational explanations, truth, and predictions is left to the form of science.

THE DUAL MEANING OF AESTHETICS

Reference to the concept "aesthetics" is often confusing, especially in relation to organizational theory. A common connotation seems to be the study of beauty. For example, most of the contributions by Guillet de Monthoux, Gustafsson, and Sjöstrand (2007) regarding "aesthetic leadership" deal with aesthetics and art as beauty or as art forms.

According to Budd (1998), the concept of aesthetics owes its name to the German philosopher Alexander Gottlieb Baumgarten (1714–1762). Baumgarten derived the name from the Greek *aisthanomai,* meaning perception by means of the senses. According to Wikipedia (2008), this revision of aesthetics is often regarded as a key moment in the history of aesthetic philosophy. With Baumgarten, the word "aesthetics" was developed to mean the study of good and bad taste, whereas it traditionally had been used in relation to sensibility and senses. The turn towards the study of beauty and taste now presented the new wealthy classes criteria they could use to distinguish between good and bad art.

So perhaps we can blame Baumgarten for the dual meaning of aesthetics. On the one hand, the original meaning encapsulates how we, in very basic and intuitive ways, experience the world through our senses. On the other hand, aesthetics has become a way of understanding art, appreciating art, and distinguishing between what may be good and bad expressions of art. These two roots are evident in Cassirer's philosophy. The original meaning is found in Cassirer's portrayal of experiencing the world through our immediate senses. The second is found in his development of symbolic forms, and his discussion of art as a specific form that carries its own illumination, angle of refraction, and implicit logics. In *An Essay on Man* (1944), Cassirer draws on Baumgarten, as he also does in *Freiheit und Form* (1916) and in *The Philosophy of the Enlightenment* ([1932] 1951).

But, as Axel Spree (2003) pointed out, Cassirer seemed to neglect some of Baumgarten's achievements, and instead presented him simply as an initial stage on the way to Kant's aesthetics. Spree's conclusion seems to be that a resemblance does exist between the theories of Cassirer and Baumgarten, but that the similarity after all is small.

What seems to be the case is that Cassirer's philosophy of symbolic forms addresses the two core meanings of aesthetics, which are, according to Malcolm Budd (1998), the philosophy of art on the one hand, and the philosophy of the aesthetic experience and character of objects or phenomena other than art on the other. The notion of symbolic forms somehow brings these two roots together, in the sense that man's consciousness is an expression of, and a consequence of, immediate sense experiences that are molded through symbolic forms that are historically and culturally developed. Consciousness is an expression of the cultural life and development of mankind, as well as an expression of the biological processes taking place in our here-and-now epistemological encounters with the world. Most neuroscientists naturally focus on the latter. Antonio Damasio is no exception, even though he relates his studies to Descartes, Spinoza, Kant, and other philosophers.

Adrian Carr (2002) pointed out that the everyday meaning and usage of the term "aesthetics" have shifted considerably over the centuries following Baumgarten. From being a systematic study of the sensual and affective dimension of human experience, aesthetics today has come to mean ways of categorizing and judging art. That is, aesthetics has become strongly related to beauty. In response to this trend, Philip Hancock (2002) expressed a strong distrust of those who champion the incorporation of aesthetic values and practices into the business world, fearing that aesthetic experience will be reduced to standardized and rationalized elements in a long tradition of corporate management.

One should then not forget that *knowing* is at the heart of aesthetics, as Taylor and Carboni (2008) remind us, and a form of knowing that we get directly from our sensory experience. Sensory experience is our primary experience and the basis for all our knowing, as well as for organizations. Thus, they call for increased research on aesthetics in organizations, claiming that the role of aesthetics has gained too little focus in organizational research.

ON NEUROSCIENCE, AESTHETIC SENSATION, AND SYMBOLIC FORMS

Damasio's account of neurobiology and the consequences for perception, learning, and ethics is intriguing. Damasio presents what I consider an important contribution to the understanding of the relationships among emotions, feelings, thinking, and action. Seen in connection to organizational theory and management education, the consequences for such areas as decision-making, learning, and ethical behavior become especially relevant.

Damasio's depiction of consciousness as developing on the basis of feelings and emotions, as well as his discussion of possible consequences for both the individual and the social systems if feelings and emotions are ruled out (Damasio 1994, 2003), is important. However, some problematics are attached. For example, Damasio heavily emphasizes the biological progress of emotions. What is missing in his account is a thorough discussion of the likely process of emotions as a result of the conscious growth and learning of the individual as a social person. The biological construction of emotions is underscored in Damasio's account, whereas the role of culture and learning in the development of emotions receives less attention. The likelihood that emotions are developed through the *historical and cultural* development of man's consciousness thus needs additional analysis, and here it seems to me that Cassirer may contribute fruitfully. For example, such symbolic forms as myth, history, science, language, and art can be used to analyze how moral development and ethical judgment take different directions, according to different forms of knowing.

Criticism of Descartes is one of many points where Damasio and Cassirer seem to agree. Although coming from different disciplines, both were spokespersons for an integrated view of aesthetic experiences and thinking, and the natural sciences and the humanities.[8] Neither calls for integration in the sense that different views are to be fused into one; rather, each calls for a combined, pluralistic view. Damasio (2003) concluded that neuroscience's elimination of emotions and feelings, a consequence of a Cartesian split, leads to an impoverishment of our understanding of man and society (159). Cassirer similarly claimed that science reduces and classifies, analyzes and scrutinizes sense objects and the study of their effects in a process of abstraction that implies an impoverishment of reality (Cassirer 1944: 149). How an aesthetic experience through immediate sensation lay the basis for thinking is another area where Damasio and Cassirer seem to agree. Damasio (1993) used the Iowa experiment to demonstrate that we apply two different strategies to make sense of the world. The first is quick and intuitive and precedes the second, which is conscious and rational. Cassirer similarly claimed that the world is given to us through immediate sensations, and through symbolic forms these impressions are allocated particular qualities and configured so that reality is constituted for us. That is, sensation precedes thinking, and rationality comes after aesthetic experience; but the process is mediated through symbolic forms.

Attempts to explain the historical development of consciousness must include consideration of certain differences between Damasio and Cassirer. Whereas Cassirer used symbolic forms as tools to elucidate culture's role in the development of consciousness, Damasio had access to modern neuroscientific tools to scrutinize the human brain. Whereas Cassirer applied symbolic forms to understand the cultural and historical expressions of man's consciousness, Damasio pointed to the significance of emotions and claimed that evolution seems to have assembled the brain machinery of emotion and feeling in installments.

In contrast, Cassirer described the historical development of man's consciousness from a cultural point of view. Science, language, art, myth, and other possible symbolic forms all are configurations towards being. They represent the main directions of our understanding insofar as they form the ideal process and shape a unity of meaning by which reality is constituted for us. The symbolic forms take our understanding in different directions and differentiate our sensory and spiritual consciousness (*PSF* 1: 107).

Both Cassirer and Damasio showed that we experience reality through our senses, through aesthetic experience. They proposed that our senses, emotions, and feelings are our interfaces towards reality. When we face a situation; sensing comes before cognition, but sensing and cognition are merely different levels of the same process. Sensation and cognition are interrelated, but sensation is "deeper," closer to the immediate reality, than cognition. Cassirer's supplementary contribution is his explanation of how our engagement with the world is mediated through symbolic forms. Neuroscience does not explain the historically developed forms of man's engagement with the world, the expressions of man's historical development of consciousness, the cultural ways of knowing represented by symbolic forms, and how these forms represent different logics and different angles of refraction.

Returning to Cassirer's discussion of the complementary qualities of the two symbolic forms science and art and considering the insights from neuroscience reveals that symbolic forms represent different logics that have developed historically. In order to understand the logics of art with its weight on interpretation and imagination, one has to turn to the humanities, whereas the essence of the symbolic form of science can most easily be identified in the natural sciences. For example, science looks for explanations, causalities, and truth; whereas art illuminates and intensifies but does not seek rational explanations, truth, and predictions. Additionally, the different angles of refraction imply that science tends to focus on the part of the epistemological process that is related to the cognitive level, whereas art is sense-based and sense-oriented, rather than rational-cognitive. Through aesthetic understanding, our perspective directs us towards the intuitive "precognitive" level—to sensing, emotions, and feelings. Through the form of art, the configuration towards being takes different paths than the molding that takes place in the form of science.

Being able to use both eyes thus means being able to "tune in" to both the aesthetic and the cognitive, and to develop the capacity to combine the different logics and levels of refractions of art and science. Doing so requires that we (a) realize something lies beneath the surface, outside the realm of science and language; (b) have at least an elementary understanding of the difference between the levels; and (c) have at least an elementary knowledge of the diverse logics that follow the different channels/symbolic forms to the dissimilar levels of the same reality and know how to apply them.

Consequently, we can learn to become two-eyed practitioners (i.e., practitioners who are capable of alternating between a scientific- or language-based and an art- aesthetic-based understanding). If this ability can be learned, and if this learning is important in order to become a good practitioner, I suggest that it should be a part of management education.

6   Bringing Cassirer into Organizations

In this chapter, I propose that both neurobiology and empirical studies of expertise mainly focus on individuals detached from formal organizational contexts. I contend that good individual practice does not necessarily secure good organizational practice. However, studies of expertise tend to show that experts are better than novices at interpreting the situation, and they have more strategies from which to choose in the situation at hand. Thus, if one wishes to educate proficient managers, it is necessary to develop the capacity to "see" organizations correctly. Doing so requires multiple forms of knowing, according to Cassirer. I discuss what Leonardo da Vinci's *Saper Vedere* (to know how to see) might imply when taken into organizations, how the eye of science and the eye of art may be combined, and the challenges we face if we want to develop management curricula that are based on the combination of science and art for which Cassirer was a spokesman.

BETWEEN RICHNESS AND SIMPLICITY

According to Cassirer, science takes us to the objective world through its specific way of organizing our sense perceptions. Science and language help us determine and establish our ideas of the external world so that we can give them accurate meaning. If we emphasize explanations, finalities, causalities, and categories, we are drawn towards the surface levels. Reaching the deeper level depends on our ability to apply the requested perspective or angle of refraction (i.e., to focus on the intuitive, on feelings and emotions, instead of ignoring it). It calls for a particular aesthetic awareness—seeing, wondering, opening up—and logics and angles other than those offered by science.

However, I maintain that it should also be possible to reach the deeper levels through an immediate, intuitive, and "natural" awareness without an understanding of the logics and consequences of art as a symbolic form. But if it stops there, we are deprived the capacity to navigate in abstract, symbolic space, such as the tribesman Cassirer uses as an illustration: an expert in navigating in concrete space, but totally lost when asked to handle abstract spatial relations (*EoM*: 46). If an immediate, straightforward channel is our only channel to reality, we are, like animals or like Mattis in Vesaas' *The Birds* (2002), confined within the world of immediate sense perceptions. To understand, and not only to be aware of, the role of the deeper level depends on knowledge of the logics that art as a symbolic form represents—knowledge about what art has to offer as a way of stretching out to and mediating reality. Art and science are generally occupied with different phenomena and in different ways. Art does not typically aim at explaining and reaching conclusions; it does not try to mirror reality, to find truths, to reduce, or to classify. Whereas art may illuminate and unveil deep phenomena, it also follows that art may be a poor channel to surface phenomena if simplification, precision, explanation, and causalities is our goal. Science is the most elaborate way to the surface level, but is unapt when it comes to gaining access to the deeper level, as depicted in Table 6.1. Science is typically not focused on deep-level phenomena such as emotions, feelings, values, imagination, and so on—this is an area of man's cultural life that seems to become peripheral for the eye of science.

If we approach deep phenomena through science's way of categorizing, classifying, and reducing, we "scientize" the deeper levels; consequently, they lose their richness. But to interpret Table 6.1 as if science cannot or should not be used at the deeper levels would be to interpret it erroneously. The eye of science may be perfectly appropriate for analyzing deep-level phenomena if it is a measured attempt to reduce complexity for the sake of simplicity. Similarly, the eye of art may help us see aspects of surface phenomena that we normally ignore when using the eye of science, if we apply "artful inquiry" (Barry 1996).

Cassirer's approach challenges us to see how the levels interact, and to use both eyes, from the perspectives of both science and art. In management education as well as in other areas of life, the first challenge then is to understand how art and science are channels that tend to draw our attention to different layers. The second is to understand how the deeper intuitive sensory and the rational cognitive processes are parts of the same process, and how art and science jointly may contribute to a more realistic experience of reality, as Cassirer promised. The third challenge is how to develop the ability to see with "two eyes." Neuroscience has explained the

Table 6.1 Different Areas of Appropriateness

	Surface level	Deep level
Art	Unapt/Peripheral(or deliberately used to create richness)	Apt/Focused
Science	Apt/Focused	Unapt/Peripheral(or deliberately used to simplify)

different layers in an integrated process between the "given world" and our cognitive rational understanding. We understand through processes where sensing, emotions, and feelings precede cognition; yet at the same time they are interrelated. However, in a world where the logics and levels of refractions of science often dominate, we tend to ignore the deeper level of sensing, emotions, and feelings. We run into habitual blindness: instead of being confined to the realm of sense perceptions, we become prisoners of rational thinking.

DIFFERENT LEVELS IN ORGANIZATIONS

The Iowa card game experiment presented in Chapter 5 illustrated how the deeper and the surface levels of consciousness interact (Gladwell 2005; Damasio 1994). The surface level is the conscious level, where the test subjects became aware of what they already had experienced bodily on a deeper level. But many levels exist between conscious reasoning and simple unconscious responses, as is illustrated in Damasio's *Levels of Life Regulation* model (Damasio 1999: 55). Here we find on the very deepest level "the survival kit," which involves relatively simple stereotyped patterns of response that we may perceive as states of pain, drive, and motivation. On a higher level, we find secondary, primary, and background emotions that are more complex but still stereotyped patterns of response. Then, just beneath the surface of unconsciousness, we find the level of feelings, where sensory patterns signaling pain, pleasure, and emotions become images. We now cross the surface and reach the level of consciousness, where we find what Damasio called "high reasoning." At this level, complex, flexible, and customized plans of response are formulated into conscious images that may be executed as behavior. Between the upper and lower levels, the causation goes both ways.

If we look for parallel models on the organizational level, theories of organizational culture come to the mind—particularly Edgar Schein's deep-level model. He too addressed the conscious and unconscious levels, describing causation as going both ways. Like Damasio, Schein (2001, 1999) emphasized the strong and subtle influence deeper levels have on surface-level behavior. But the differences between Damasio and Schein are obvious. Most noticeably, Damasio focused on the individual, whereas Schein focused on the collective. Additional differences become evident in Schein's often-cited definition:

> The culture of a group can now be defined as: A pattern of shared basic assumptions that the group learned as it solved its problems of external adaptation and internal integration, that has worked well enough to be considered valid and therefore, to be taught to new members as the correct way to perceive, think, and feel in relation to those problems.
>
> (Schein 2001: 373–374)

Both Damasio and Schein were concerned with external adaption. But whereas Damasio was occupied with biological responses, emotions, and feelings on the unconscious levels, Schein pointed to basic and taken-for-granted assumptions and values on the collective level.

The deep-level cultural theorists claim that causation exists where underlying assumptions may become "out of sight" as taken-for-granted systems of knowledge shared by a group of people (Gudykunst and Kim 1992). This "quiet" system of knowledge may structure the group's notions of reality and govern how they see the world (Littlejohn 1992). When a culture becomes settled, we find in its heart a shared ideology that offers prescriptions for a way of life (Wilden 1987). Settled cultures are not in open competition with alternative models for organizing experience. However, they do have " . . . the undisputed authority of habit, normality, and common sense" (Swidler 1986: 281). A dominant organizational ideology as a set of ideas in residence has achieved local hegemony (Czarniawska 1997), infusing everyday experience and blending unnoticeably into common-sense assumptions about what is true. A taken-for-granted standard is established, and people naturally "know" how to act (Swidler 1986).

As a cultural philosopher, Cassirer added to this picture his theory of symbolic forms. Symbolic forms have different angles of refraction and ways of mediating reality. Science tends to concentrate on surface-level phenomena, whereas art focuses on deep-level phenomena. What then regularly falls outside their respective focus when applied to, and in, organizations? What, for example, will we see most clearly when we apply the eye of science to organizational phenomena? Cassirer claimed that science is dependent on classification and categorization, and focuses on causalities and finalities. Damasio claimed that "proper" neuroscientific research has been directed towards that which appeared objective and concrete and has shunned feelings and other phenomena that appear to be too subjective and indefinable for studies of the brain.

If Cassirer's and Damasio's claims are valid, it follows that the focal point of management science is the phenomena that can most easily be identified, numbered, and counted. It is first and foremost the material world or the phenomena that can be objectified and treated as identifiable entities, so that they are easy to handle and even fit into mathematical models (Ghoshal 2005: 81). Accordingly; the more "messy" phenomena are left to interpretive research. These are the phenomena that Damasio claims neuroscience traditionally has avoided: emotions, feelings, values, and (we may add) mental pictures, paradigmatic assumptions, and hidden power relations.

However, to illustrate the different realms of science and art by means of a cultural model alone would be much too simple. First of all, as already indicated in previous chapters, the distinction between science and art cannot be drawn sharply between the surface level and the deep level. Management science (measured or not) also deals with deep phenomena, and interpretive research and artful inquiry often deal with surface phenomena.

A second reason for not basing analysis on cultural models alone is that it easily leaves out an area where management science often hands the responsibility for surface phenomena to over to aesthetic and artistic inquiry—namely, when creativity is on the agenda (Adler 2006; Augier 2004).

But I do propose that it is correct to say that the eye of science, first and foremost, tends to be attracted to the phenomena at the organizational surface level, and the eye of art tends to lean toward deep-level phenomena and to potential areas for creative innovation and artistic inquiry. One should then bear in mind that "the eye of science" and "the eye of art" refer to more than theories and methods; they refer to symbolic forms. Symbolic forms are levels of consciousness and culturally and historically developed ways of knowing that guide the actors' (researchers' as well as managers') attention and provide them with tools with which to think as well as act. In order to develop organizational expertise, we need to go beyond the limitations of single forms of knowing, if we are to take Cassirer seriously.

In the following, we therefore turn to studies of expertise, and from there take expertise into the context of formal organizations in order to understand the role of symbolic forms in developing proficient managers.

EXPERTS AT WORK

As already illustrated, both Cassirer and the neurobiologists claim that cognition, rational thinking, and logical interpretation take place against a background of intuitive sensory understanding. Both also point to the importance of sensation, feelings, and immediate experiences in the way we operate in daily life. Summarizing a series of experiments, Gladwell (2005) concluded that we have underestimated the instantaneous impressions and conclusions that spontaneously arise when we confront complex situations and new people. He explains it as "thin slicing," or " . . . the ability of our unconscious to find patterns in situations and behavior based on very narrow slices of experience" (Gladwell 2005: 23). [1]

Gladwell (2005) believes that experts are aware of the importance of what goes on behind the locked door of their unconsciousness (179). They also seem adept at tuning in to others' lifeworlds, at combining facts and words with emotional and intuitive communication. Gladwell exemplifies this claim with a series of scientific experiments, as well as cases from everyday situations. For example, in the U.S. the risk of being sued for malpractice has little to do with the number of mistakes a doctor makes. Analysis of malpractice lawsuits showed that some doctors who made mistakes were never sued; however, some highly skilled doctors were often sued. Analysis revealed that patients do not file lawsuits because of mistakes alone, but because of how their doctor treated them on a personal level. For example, Levinson et al. (1997) studied hundreds of conversations between patients and doctors; they found that the physicians who had never been sued spent more than three minutes longer with each patient than those who had been sued. Primary care physicians who had been sued at least twice spent an average of 15 minutes with their patients; those who had never been sued spent an average of 18.3 minutes with their patients. As for content, the first group were more likely to do framing, orienting patients more, and explaining what they were about to do during the examination. They more actively listened, encouraging their patients to reveal more about their understanding of their situation. Compared with the doctors who had been sued, they did not reveal more facts and details about the condition of the patient or the medication. "The difference was entirely in *how* they talked to the patients" (Gladwell 2005: 42).

Essentially, Gladwell confirmed the findings of such prominent contributors as Dreyfus, Dreyfus, and Athanasiou (1986); Dreyfus and Dreyfus (2005); Schön (1987, 1991); and Csikszentmihalyi (1990): the hallmark of good practitioners is the ability to sense what is going on here and now, and to cope with a complex situation without having to stop and analyze the problem rationally.

This professional competence is often regarded as a special "sense" or a special way of "seeing," following Gladwell. Some surgeons have an extraordinary diagnostic talent, and find a tumor that others could not find. Brilliant generals possess *coup d'oeil*: with only a quick survey or glance, they are capable of maneuvering in ways that surprise the enemy. Some tennis players have "court sense" and are in the right place to reach "impossible" balls that their opponents are sure will be out of reach. Good soccer players show a feel for the game and instinctively know where to move on the field.[2] In the classroom, some teachers intuitively feel when something is wrong, or when their message does not come through. At work, some managers seem capable of "reading" what is about to happen before the decision's dysfunctional effect actually manifests in the form of red numbers.

Experts sometimes describe being in a state of flow, Csikszentmihalyi (1990) maintained. The person is in what Csikszentmihalyi coined an *autotelic* situation, driven by an internal motivation that is fueled by the situation and the challenges at hand. Flow is experienced as a feeling of being "in the zone" and at one with the activity. No analytical distance exists between the individual and the activities that individual is performing. Brothers Hubert and Stuart Dreyfus' (2005) depiction of expertise follows a similar line of thought. Their staircase of development begins with the novice, followed by the advanced beginner, competence, proficiency, and—at the fifth and highest level—expertise:

> The proficient performer, immersed in the world of skillful activity, sees what needs to be done, but decides how to do it. The expert not only sees what needs to be achieved: thanks to a vast repertoire of

situational discriminations, he or she also sees immediately how to achieve the goal.

(Dreyfus and Dreyfus 2005: 787)

The intuitive feeling of the situation, the ability to interpret the situation quickly and correctly, is the very trademark of the expert. "The expert driver not only feels in the seat of his pants when speed is the issue; he knows how to perform the appropriate action without calculating and comparing alternatives" (Dreyfus and Dreyfus 2005: 787). Schön described similar situations when portraying what he called "professional artists," saying that a sort of improvisation takes place when the professional is "reflecting-in-action" (Schön 1987, 1991).

SOME CRITICAL NOTES ON EXPERTISE

Critical voices have been heard. For example, Higgins (2001) claimed that reflection can take forms other than those that Schön described, and criticized Schön as being too instrumental. Selinger and Crease (2002) claimed that we could imagine a nearly perfect society if Dreyfus was right, and asked why societies are endangered by experts.

My own critique is somewhat different. I do not question that experts are better than novices at interpreting a situation and that they have a larger repertoire of strategies on which to draw. Rather, my concerns are based on my wish to develop good work *within organizational contexts,* primarily formal work organizations. What I have found are studies of individual expertise detached from formal institutional contexts. We cannot, however, assume that what constitutes good individual professional practice also contributes to good *organizational* practice. As a business training and development manager, I learned that even the best specialist may fail in a complex and uncertain organizational context. I have, for example, seen engineers with top grades from reputable universities do brilliant analysis in front of their computers and then fail miserably when trying to take their analysis across their own office doorstep—and then blame the organization. Hence, a celebration of expertise as individual characteristics alone will not do when we are trying to understand good work in formal organizational contexts.

First, as I have already noted, the celebration of the experts stems mainly from studies of *individual* practice. Many of the examples depict chess players, drivers, and performing artists deeply involved in the tasks at hand. Other actors may be present, but what we have observed is mainly individual competency exhibited in professional or artistic practice. When studies involve groups and organizations, they tend to be informal and directly observable, such as a team of players. We rarely see examples that are based on practice in formal and bureaucratic organizations; if they are, they tend to limit analysis to the individual level and the situation here and now.

Second, the potential aggregated effects that may surface at later stages in an organization are seldom discussed. Expertise and professional artistry are described as focused on the here and now. Typically the best practitioners are described as "becoming one with the situation." Schön (1987) opened up to some degree by describing professional artistry as "reflection-in-action", but the focus on the here and now is still strong. When one applies an organizational perspective to the celebration of individual expertise, myopia and suboptimalization soon become evident (Levinthal and March 1993). That is, the solution to a problem here and now may create serious problems at later stages in the work process or in other departments. Thus, expertise as described by Dreyfus, Schön, and Csikszentmihalyi is a local intelligence that is short-sighted (Weick 1993: 373).

Third, ruling out rational calculating, rules, and facts (the main interest of management science) from expertise is problematic in organizations that build on formal and bureaucratic logics. Formal work organizations are attempts to institutionalize standardized sets of responses to problems where rule-following is essential (March and Simon 1958; Tsoukas and Chia 2002). The problematic status of improvisation in formal organizations reflects this collision between different logics. Even the most astonishing improvisation may be a potential threat to safety, security, and productivity. This Janus-faced aspect of individual expertise does not disappear by unilaterally celebrating individual professional artistry.

It is my opinion that the conclusions from the studies of experts compared to novices are not wrong; they merely ignore the effect of institutional forms and the institutional pressure that formal bureaucratic organizations expel on their actors. If the ability to "see" the situation quickly and correctly is a hallmark of expertise, one of the implications is that experts need to expand their area of expertise to include the particularities of an institutional context. The expert needs to learn to "see" the organization. On the basis of his own research on experts, as well as his review of other studies, Berliner (1994, 2004) characterized experts as having better, richer, deeper, and more functional representations of the situation. Compared to novices, they more accurately interpret cues and are better at recognizing patterns. The ability to "see" the situation reduces the experts' cognitive load and makes them better at predicting.

The ability to interpret the organization, to read complex situations, and to predict what might happen is probably the most sought-after capacity in complex and dynamic organizations. Any manager or employee possessing such competencies would be highly valued. How to develop this capacity would likewise be of great value. Once again we turn to Cassirer and his claims that good practice requires the use of several forms of knowing.

TRANSCENDING DICHOTOMIES AND
APPROACHING ORGANIZATIONAL REALITY

In contrast with hermeneutic philosophy as represented by Gadamer (1989) and others, Cassirer claimed that we may gain an understanding of the world outside the realm of language. To Gadamer, man is a linguistic being who makes his experiences within the frames of language. We are not capable of reaching understanding without already being in "the dimension of the word"; we cannot express any particular utterance about this reality independent of ourselves, unless it has already gone through a process of articulation (Gadamer 1981: 38). Cassirer, on the other hand, did not deny that we achieve knowledge of the world within the dimension of language, but he claimed that language (or science) is just one way of gaining a more objective and realistic view of the world, through classification of our sense perceptions. Language is merely one of many symbolic forms that mold our understanding. The process that takes place through language is different from the process of art, and resembles the scientific process. Language and science both imply classification, which necessarily involves abstraction; because abstraction is an impoverishment of reality, language and science are not enough to give us a sufficiently rich, practical, and more objective view of the world. Art has other strengths and characteristics. Here Cassirer found support in John Dewey ([1934] 2005), who claimed that art " . . . is a mode of prediction not found in charts and statistics, and it insinuates possibilities of human relations not to be found in rule and precept, admonition and administration" (363). Art becomes a necessary way to cope with reality, not something esoterically disconnected from daily life practice.

It is worth noting that Cassirer argued for a more objective view, and he did not claim that reality could be found as absolute truth. He was not an absolutist, in the sense that a mimetic representational view of knowledge lay behind his philosophy. Our knowledge of reality does not mirror reality. The symbolic forms represent the ideal process by which reality is constituted for us as one and many (*PSF* 1: 107). However, Cassirer was a pragmatist in the sense that he perceived science and art as two different channels that may bring us closer to reality. There are layers of reality, and the deeper layers are gradually hidden through the development of habitual blindness. The role of art is the illumination of the hidden layers. Through art, we may achieve a more objective view, but Cassirer did not claim that we will reach a totally objective view. Art may illuminate and intensify hidden aspects of reality, but it cannot provide us with absolute truth. Art can never become a replica or imitation of a ready-made, prearranged reality; but it offers ways leading to a more realistic view of things and of human life, Cassirer seems to promise.

Cassirer fell between different poles, and in particular between the poles of *Naturwissenschaften* and *Geisteswissenschaften*. Cassirer argued against Heidegger's radical phenomenology, as he did against the Vienna circle of logical empiricists. In a discourse dominated by the antagonistic philosophical schools, it became difficult to categorize Cassirer. The development of philosophy in general and organizational thought in particular after Cassirer's death seems to have continued this antagonism. The rational approaches of organization theory, with a focus on concrete surface phenomena with formal plans, quantitative objectives, and hierarchical organizational structures, stand in contrast to the interpretive view of organization as deep-level phenomena with values, norms, sense-making, interpretations, feelings, and mental images as the main areas of interest. The ontological and epistemological assumptions underlying these two directions represent different views of knowledge as truth and facts versus "process" and relations. Management tends to become either programming and control or adaptation, exploration, learning, and symbolic management, depending on which ontological and epistemological assumptions guide the focus.

When making a case for art as supplementing the dominating eye of science, Cassirer pointed to the power of artistic imagination. Art as one of many symbolic forms is a way of engaging with the world, where one of the strengths of art is the ability to illuminate the multileveled reality. In Chapter 3, we saw how art in business is often used as decoration, entertainment, instruments for facilitation, or part of the transformation process (Darsø 2004). Cassirer's approach was more profound, in the sense that he presented art as a form of knowing that may help us attain a more objective view of the world, in particular when it is combined with science. If we apply Cassirer's optometric metaphor to organizations, the eye of art makes it possible to go beyond the formal structures of organizational life. Combined with science, we may then apply art to develop a three-dimensional view of organizations. For example, all of the four functions of art in business as described by Darsø may be approached in both scientific and artistic ways (i.e., by applying the symbolic form of science or the symbolic form of art). If we choose to understand decoration by applying the logics and levels of refractions of science, we are more attracted to other aspects than we are if we apply the lens of art. However, the use of "both eyes" on organizational phenomenon makes it possible to understand how the surface levels and the deeper levels of these phenomena interact. This need to develop a capacity to cope with the world in a binocular way is the core of Cassirer's message.

BEYOND THE ORGANIZATIONAL SURFACE

The deep structure of organizations has been discussed by such scholars as Pondy (1978, 1989), Deetz and Kersten (1983), and Putnam (1983). This deep structure consists of phenomena that are of utmost importance to management. However, for several reasons they seem to fall outside the realm of our daily perception (Putnam 1983). One obvious reason is the not-so-obvious ontological status of the deep structure. The phenomena hidden in the deep structure take the form of individual and collective values, norms, power relations, beliefs, attitudes, mindsets, cognitive and shared maps, deep ideology, and paradigmatic assumptions. These phenomena do not have the same concrete form or immediate appearance as the manifest behavior and objects on the surface level. Another reason that they seem to fall outside the territory of our daily perception is the very status of the surface phenomena in the field of management. The apparent behavior of actors, technology, written accounts, formal structures (e.g., charts, procedures, routines), and other surface phenomena are positioned in the very focus of traditional organizational theory and practice.

Central location and dominant status help surface phenomena attract our attention, and their significance as well as their immediate appearance easily leads our concentration away from the deeper structure. Thus, in a sense, the surface structure rests on the deep structure. Its dominant position is dependent on the fact that the deep structure continues to be concealed (Putnam 1983). The very moment we reveal the existence of the deep structure and start discussing its meaning, the manifest surface phenomena may lose their dominant position. For example, if the actions and goals of an implementation plan are analyzed in light of their underlying governing values, an illumination of the plan's action logics may reveal that the intentions may be built on assumptions that are not valid. Or if the hidden power structures in a management group are brought to the surface, the surface behavior of the actors may dramatically change. Or if the shared values of an organization change, the new dominant organizational ideology may revolutionize not only the way people think about their organization and their work, but also the way they actually perform.

Such changes do not come easily. If a management team collectively enhances its ability to see with both eyes, the taken-for-granted position of conventional ways of planning and decision-making is challenged. Turning from a one-eyed to a two-eyed view is therefore also a question of altering the power balance because it challenges the established ideology in residence.

FROM ONE-EYED TO TWO-EYED MANAGEMENT

Where has this discussion led thus far? Here is my attempt to encapsulate some essentials in the form of propositions regarding implications for organization in general and management in particular.

Proposition 1: The deep phenomena have a strong and often subtle influence on the manifest phenomena at the organizational surface level.

An acknowledgement of the very existence of these phenomena is necessary in order to improve practice. Ignorance of the deep phenomena prevents a learning process that could lead to a more profound and realistic knowledge of organizational processes. In order to learn, we first must acknowledge that there is actually something to seek behind the surface, and then we need the ability to see what is there.

Proposition 2: When the deep phenomena fall outside our daily perception, we lose not only a deeper insight into the realm of organizational life, but also the ability to make a deep impact on organizational practice.

Thus, we need to develop an understanding of how deep phenomena affect the surface level and how organizational practice can be productively influenced through affecting these phenomena.

Proposition 3: The two levels of surface and deep structure are interrelated and constitute each other: they represent different aspects of the same reality, rather than two independent worlds.

Therefore, it is important that we develop the relational and processual ability to see how organizational phenomena are multileveled, and how they may "move" in and between different layers of organizational space.

Proposition 4: Turning from one-eyed to two-eyed management challenges the dominant organizational ideology in residence.

If one eye is dominant, the logics and focus of this peculiar form of knowing will be materialized into tools, technology, and taken-for granted ways of working and thinking. An attempt to turn towards two-eyed management will consequently be unsuccessful if the intention is not merely to change the way we "see" organizations, but also to change the current practice.

Proposition 5: Educating two-eyed managers is a field in which much is left to do.

The eye of science still dominates management education. When art-based and aesthetic views are included in the curricula, it is often in the form of additional and creative courses or techniques to solve business problems or induce innovation. Creative art-based techniques and out-of-the box thinking are typically employed when the eye of science proves to be too restrictive.

These propositions illustrate the challenges of bringing plural forms of knowing into management education and practice. First, one has to realize that the surface and the deep structure represent different aspects of the same reality. Then one has to learn how science may help us see the surface world, and how art may help us see the deeper levels. The main challenge still remains: finding ways to develop the ability to see both dimensions of reality at the same time in order to see the whole, three-dimensional picture and thus a more objective and practical view of organizational life.

Cassirer used the idea of binocular vision when he illustrated the need to use both eyes simultaneously. The practicality of a three-dimensional view of the world is demonstrated in the field of optometry: a binocular vision is the result of both eyes working together simultaneously, accurately, and complementarily. The separate images from the two eyes are combined into three-dimensional images in the brain. Such stereo vision gives us depth perception, the ability to see three-dimensional space. This ability is of immense practical importance. With binocular depth perception, we are able to judge visually the relative distances between objects; we gain a more accurate perception of how people and things are moving in the space. Thus, we can relate time to space, and to larger extent we can predict what is going to happen next. In other words, binocular vision is necessary for us to obtain the deeper insight that makes it possible to move accurately and effectively in three-dimensional space. The same should apply to the practice of management. If managers relate to the surface structures alone, they are hindered in a similar way as people suffering from such binocular vision disabilities as amblyopia ("lazy eye") or strabismus ("crossed eye," "wall eye," or "wandering eye"). The consequence could be difficulty navigating in complex and changing contexts.

Eye misalignments are in some cases not evident to the untrained observer. Such may be the case with one-eyed management as well. We may not see it in the way people look or in how they behave in normal situations where they control their surroundings. We may, however, get an indication when the context changes and the fixed points are fewer, as in periods where organizational change creates discontinuity and flux. The same managers may then display serious difficulty in understanding the dynamics and in navigating under the changed conditions.

Metaphors may appear useful, but they also have limitations. Binocular vision disabilities can be cured through exercises focusing on eye teaming, focusing, acuity (clarity of sight), binocular coordination, and depth perception. Likewise, single vision among managers, whether they tend to focus on only the surface or on the deep level, can probably be treated. But this treatment is more profound because it requires a form of learning that is different from correcting neurophysiologic or neurosensory visual dysfunctions.

THE DOMINANT POSITION OF THE ORGANIZATIONAL SURFACE

One challenge in using both eyes lies in the undisputed position of science. Cassirer claimed that the concept of science did not exist before the great Greek thinkers, and then it seemed to be forgotten until it was rediscovered and reestablished in the Age of the Renaissance. Thereafter, the triumph of science was absolute and uncontested, according to Cassirer (1944), and it stands as the most important power in the modern world. Organizational theory and practice are certainly not exempt: science has a strong grasp on organization theory and management practice. Even before Frederick Winslow Taylor coined his theories "scientific management," science had a strong hold on management thinking (Taylor 1911). And we do need the eye of science in our organizing practices. Science gives us, among other things, an assurance of a constant world. In a shifting universe, scientific thought fixes the points of rest and creates the unmovable poles, according to Cassirer (1944). Science has, for example, helped us fix the processes of organizing and named it organization. Science gives us categories and tools with which to analyze causal relationships and to predict future consequences of current actions. This somewhat crude simplification and reduction of complex contexts may be helpful in providing something stable and easily identifiable, to which we can relate.

However, this simplification is too static. Weick (1993) made it clear that we would benefit from viewing organizations as ongoing activities rather than unmovable poles and that we should regard organizations as verbs instead of nouns. Organizing involves a diversity of activities that create networks of people, resources, tasks, technology, and other aspects of social action and interaction. The very same networks create what we tend to fix in shapes we call organizations. Managing is one of these activities, and teamwork is another. In these networks, specific processes become interrelated and difficult to differentiate. Managing is teamwork, and teamwork is managing. Formal managers (the actors appointed or assigned to certain formal positions or tasks) become performers of management. At the same time, management is practiced by actors who are not formally assigned to do so. Whether managers by name or not, all engage in formal and informal activities, weaving both formal and informal nets. They engage in ongoing organizing, where surface and deep structures are continually created and recreated. The actors become practitioners of organizing as they struggle to manage the processes of creating guiding structures in the indiscriminate mass or the stream of floating sensuous phenomena of which they are a part.

In short, the actors become explorers as well as constructors of organizing networks that take form and create forms that are intertwined surface-structural and deep-level phenomena. The surface of organizations consists of phenomena that are relatively concrete and easy to identify and observe. Here we find organizational charts, flow diagrams, value statements, written rules, policies and procedures, technology, and behavior of actors that can be observed directly and easily attract the attention of the eye of science. Even though the phenomena on the organizational surface are the easiest to identify, they often achieve a taken-for-granted status and gradually fall out of sight. The basis and premises upon which the deep-level structures rest are the most difficult to discover, but sometimes surface in crises and under uncertainty.

HEALING THE BLIND EYE OF MANAGEMENT?

How can Cassirer help us illuminate and (re)discover the different levels of organizations and how they interrelate? Cassirer argued that we need to see into the deep structure as well as the surface structure of life, if we want to see the whole picture and become skillful practitioners. Applied to the practice of organizing, this implies that organizational practitioners in general and managers in particular will benefit from discovering the forms of things behind their empirical properties, in the jargon of Cassirer. The deeper insight that may take us behind the formal structures of organizations is dependent on the development of a conceptual depth as well as a purely visual depth. The first is discovered by science; the second is revealed in art, according to Cassirer. Science helps managers discover the reason of things and the causality of processes. It creates order, hierarchies, categories, and numbers that are helpful in establishing the sense of controlled processes and the quantitative measures that are imperative in business, whether we like it or not. However, if managers tend to concentrate on causality, finality, and formal structures, they will also habitually lose sight of the immediate appearances of organizations. This reality blindness must then be healed if learning with consequences for practice is to take place. Cassirer claimed that art may offer this indispensable illumination.

Cassirer's philosophy of art and science speaks to practice in general. I believe, however, that Cassirer is particularly relevant to organizational practice, because organizations are multileveled and easily can be depicted as consisting of surface and deep structures. The formal sides of organizations are well-established and seem to have gained a dominant position in theory as well as in practice. If these claims are valid, it follows that there is a need for training managers to use their "artistic eye." Then managers may develop a richer, more profound, vivid, and colorful representation of organizations—in short, a more *realistic* view. Some management programs have answered this call and brought art into their curriculum. We already have programs that have managers learning improvisation from jazz, creativity from painters, and teamwork from actors. This is, however, not sufficient, if we follow Cassirer.

This assertion is in line with my own experience as a former in-house organizational consultant. When I brought artists into the company (and many artists are certainly convinced they can contribute to management development), they often "saw" what we, the insiders, did not easily notice. But they were usually blind when it came to identifying the formal and structural sides of the organization; in other words, they were not skilled in using a scientific eye on an organization. They lacked the eye of management science that gives name to the surface structures, and they lacked the ability to identify causalities and finalities in an organizational context. In that sense, many artists are just as one-eyed as many managers are. And when it comes to understanding formal bureaucratic organizations, I believe they are probably even more blind if they do not have a trained eye of science because the context is so different from that of a theatre troupe or a jazz group.

Thus, merely bringing art into management training programs or into organizations is not enough. According to Cassirer, what managers need is to develop their capacity to use both eyes. The third dimension of organizational space is revealed through the trained use of both eyes. Managers need to develop the decisive capacity to differentiate between the "real" and the "possible." Innovation and creative change require the ability to see what is not yet there and then to give it form. The strength of art is the power of artistic imagination and creation. To see what is not yet there and then to give it form, managers need to see the world in a new light. Even a blind deaf-mute may develop a new insight into the world. An artist may benefit from developing the eye of science in order to practice as a manager or an organizational change facilitator. For most managers, the eye of science is more fully developed than the eye of art. Accordingly, the crucial ability to differentiate between what is and what is yet to be created is constrained.

Many managers thus need training that makes them capable of breaking out of taken-for-granted frames. An idea of what the first step may be is the Brechtian *Verfremdungseffect* (the art of alienation or "making strange") in play. The German dramatist and stage director Bertolt Brecht (1898–1956) imposed on his audience a critical detachment from a play and its performance. Applied to the life of organizations, everyday phenomena can be "made strange" by applying atypical angles to the subject. Brecht's idea was not to bring the audience away from the performance or reality on stage, but to help the audience avoid being seduced by the players and the text. As a writer and director, he was teaching his audience to adopt a more critical way of seeing reality.

Ken Darnell
February 5, 1974

Having completed the original course, Ken produced this drawing about a year later.

Figure 6.1   Improving practice (Betty Edwards).[3]

In order to break out of the taken-for-granted perspectives for the purpose of developing organizational expertise, two steps must be taken. The first step is to develop the process of seeing in a new light, of attentiveness. The next step is the process of creating what is not yet there—that is, to act in a productive manner. This sequence of seeing before practicing is essential to Betty Edwards, the author of Drawing on the Right Side of the Brain (1979), who has helped adults around the world learn to draw. Learning to draw is actually not that difficult, according to Edwards; however, we must first learn how to see the world in a new light. Doing so may be a challenge for many managers as well as fine art students. Adults may be trapped in taken-for-granted forms and perspectives that restrict the capacity to practice in more effective ways. Thus, if in a learning situation we start by practicing a new technique, we will probably not experience any significant breakthrough. Accordingly, Edwards "forced" her students to alter their perspectives, transcend categories, and go beyond surface structures. The result was astonishing, as Figure 6.1 illustrates. Her students clearly became better practitioners by learning how to see before learning techniques. If these learning effects could be achieved in management training, the result would be truly impressive.

SAPER VEDERE: LEARNING TO SEE BEFORE
LEARNING TO USE TECHNIQUES

Criticism against the dominant Anglo-Saxon organizational theory rooted in the analytic philosophical tradition, also known as the North American Theory of Organization (NATO), has been strong. According to Ghoshal (2005), we have adopted the "scientific" approach of trying to discover patterns and laws and tried to replace all notions of human intentionality with a firm belief in causal determinism to explain all aspects of corporate performance.

> In effect, we have professed that business is reducible to a kind of physics in which even if individual managers do play a role, it can safely be taken as determined by the economic, social, and psychological laws that inevitably shape peoples' actions.
>
> (Ghoshal 2005: 77)

Though I enthusiastically buy into Ghoshal's arguments, I have in this piece of writing also made a case for the necessity of functional (which Ghoshal called scientific) approaches to organization. I have also, primarily through my references to Ernst Cassirer, tried to illustrate that it is not a question of choosing one or the other approach, but in fact of choosing both.

Analyzing the interaction between the surface level and the deep level is a challenge. They represent different forms of knowledge. How these forms of knowledge constitute each other and shape different practices has to be seen and understood before intelligent actions can be taken to prevent unwanted consequences. As Brown and Duguid's (2000) analysis revealed, the celebration of official standards for organizing may result in noncanonical practices that are driven "underground"; thus, important knowledge about how to handle local problems and specific tasks is hidden from management. The official standards on the surface level disguise the unofficial behavior as well as the practical knowledge on the deep level. For reflective action to be taken, it is then a prerequisite to be able to see how both forms of knowledge and practices exist simultaneously on different levels, and how these practices interact and shape aggregated organizational behavior.

How canonical and noncanonical knowledge feeds practices that are simultaneously solving and creating problems is one of many managerial challenges that involve a need for an organizational three-dimensional view. It is also important to see how the interplay between the surface level (formal decisions, goals, plans, and apparent behavior) and deep-level phenomena (values, norms, and ideology) create organizational commitment in various forms; how structural control (control activity on the surface level) interrelates with cultural control (through ideology and values) to form organizational control; how organizational structures may lead to emotional responses such as guilt, caution, and blame; and how formal decision-making processes challenge informal decision-making processes and vice versa, resulting in intended as well as unintended consequences.

These examples illustrate processes in organizations where managers and teachers of management, according to my own experience, often tend to see only one aspect or layer of reality. In my opinion, Cassirer's call for developing art as a complement to science in order to see and navigate in three-dimensional space can help us deal more effectively with these types of real organizational challenges. "Seeing" in Cassirer's use of the word must then be understood in a broad sense. In his discussions, Cassirer also addressed such concepts as revelation, visualizing, insight, discovery, consciousness, illumination, and intensification.

Essentially, we must develop attentiveness to preconceptual layers in our engagement with the world, the processes, and the phenomena that exist before we apply names, concepts, categories, classes, numbers, indexes, and measures to them; this process takes different directions through different symbolic forms. Attaining this awareness may be a precondition for developing an actionable knowledge that may turn us into professional artists. This awareness is of particular importance under uncertainty and dynamic complexity where the pre-given plans have lost their predictive power.

Whenever we have no blueprint to tell us in detail what to do, we must work artfully, according to Austin and Devin (2003: xxii). Leonardo da Vinci (1452–1519) is an example of such a *practitioner extraordinaire,* but he did not rely on art alone. He used the term *Saper Vedere* (to know how to see) to explain his unique painting and sculpturing skills. To da Vinci, every phenomenon perceived was an object of inquiry, and seeing was the most important way to understand the facts of experience. Because he was an extraordinary artist as well as a scientist, art and science became two sides of the same coin: da Vinci was artistic as a scientist, and scientific as an artist. The ability to act towards reality in both ways at the same time gave him an extraordinary gateway to reality; therefore, he became an extraordinary practitioner.

Organization practitioners are not "da Vincis." Managers, for example, work under different conditions; their "products" are not the same as those of artists; and the quality of their work is assessed in other ways. But when habitual blindness gradually develops and limits our awareness of the surface phenomena, concepts, and categories, knowing how to see (*Saper Vedere*) becomes pertinent for practitioners as well as scholars of organization.

Managers who are learning are adult learners. Like most adults, most managers are already trained and educated in a technical-rational tradition with roots in positivistic science (Schön 1983). We have all learned to follow scripts, rules, and procedures that have been developed for standard situations, or at least for situations that we perceive as sufficiently similar for us to apply them. These scripts have typically focused on the surface level of organizations. Art may help us transcend these limitations, but we still have a long way to go before we are able to develop management curricula that are based on the combination of science and art that Cassirer proposed. We still have to understand what it really implies to "see" organizations in a binocular way, and how it can be learned (and taught); how habitual organizational blindness can be cured; how we can "see" organizations with a scientific and an artistic eye, simultaneously; and how we can develop actionable knowledge based on a combination of science and art in order to become skillful practitioners of organizing.

THE CONDEMNATION OF MANAGEMENT SCIENCE

Cassirer studied natural sciences and mathematics as well as humanities in a broad sense (history, literature, philosophy, and art). Both foundational and epistemological subjects were in his interest. He played a mediating role between *Naturwissenschaften* and *Geisteswissenschaften,* between the continental and analytic philosophical schools, between Heidegger's radical phenomenology on the one side and the Vienna circle of logical empiricists on the other. As a mediator and bridge-builder between different traditions and schools of thought, he did not gain the attention that he certainly deserved. The fact that he was a Jew in Germany and that he moved to England, then to Sweden, and finally to the U.S., where he died in 1945, is probably also a reason for the relatively modest reputation he gained outside philosophy. Many of his works have still not been translated from German, and in organizational and management theory he is hardly ever mentioned.[4]

However, the dichotomies of philosophy between which Cassirer elegantly moved are clearly evident in sociology in general and in organizational theory in particular (Emirbayer 1997; Putnam 1983). As Emirbayer pointed out, we struggle with dualisms between material versus ideal, structure versus agency, and individual versus society. We also struggle with those between spectator and participant, positivist and constructivist, explanation and understanding, manifest content and latent content, subject and object, fact and interpretation, knowledge as object and knowledge as process, and system and lifeworld. These dichotomies often disguise the relational aspects between the two sides in practical life. In this piece of writing, I contend that we need to transcend such dichotomies in order to understand organizations better, not in the sense that an amalgamation should be sought, but rather in order to investigate the possibilities of reaching a richer and more realistic understanding of organizations and management through various forms of knowing. I further maintain that Cassirer's ideas offer an explanatory power that is well-suited to the analysis of organizations. Even more, my own experiences in educating managers as well as in acting as a change agent have helped me realize that Cassirer's ideas present a relational and processual approach that practitioners often find challenging, useful, and surprisingly down-to-earth. Or, as Cassirer described it, as an approach that is close to reality.

We have seen that the criticism of management learning and education has been strong over the last few years. Three of its sharpest critics have been Sumantra Ghoshal (2005), Henry Mintzberg (2004), and Barbara Czarniawska (2003). Czarniawska, for example, points to a "forbidden knowledge" in the management curricula, and claims that most of the curricula propagate modernist ideas of control and masculine ideas of mastery. These theories build on rational myths and steer clear of organizational knowledge that offers insight and reflection on the practices of organizing. Despite their shortcomings, they are preferable to the theories that build on what Czarniawska calls "forbidden knowledge."

Czarniawska (2003) depicts a divided world consisting of the good and the bad. So does Henry Mintzberg (2004). "The problem today, increasingly, is that we have two cultures—specifically, two very different approaches to the process of managing," Henry Mintzberg (2004) claimed in his hard-hitting allegation against MBAs (128). He depicted a war between the professional culture and the entrepreneurial culture, where the first emphasizes security, order, and formality, and the second focuses on the informal, practical, and uncertain. In the professional culture, MBAs are taught to analyze and calculate, to create spreadsheets, and to close deals; they tend to be distant, elitist, and self-focused once they are employed by a company. Mintzberg (2004) advocated the development of a more entrepreneurial culture through the use of theories and teaching in order to generate more thoughtful reflection on experience (253). The goal is then to develop managers that are capable of becoming reflective practitioners (Schön 1983, 1987).

Mintzberg's and Czarniawska's portrayals of two antagonistic traditions parallel Sumantra Ghoshal's (2005) allegation that management theories are " . . . overwhelmingly causal or functional in their modes of explanation" (78). We are, according to Ghoshal, teaching and applying bad management theories that are destroying good management practices. We do not teach theories that are more realistic because such a perspective cannot be elegantly modeled. It is not based on mathematics; it does not make sharp, testable propositions or simple prescriptions possible. If we did teach these theories, business could not be treated as what we perceive as science, and we would fall back on the wisdom of common sense—that is, a wisdom that combines "what is" with "what ought to be"—to develop practical understanding and pragmatic prescriptions, Ghoshal (2005) somewhat sarcastically claimed (81).

Ghoshal, Mintzberg, and Czarniawska pictured an organizational world divided in two antagonistic traditions. This approach is, as we have seen in Chapter 4, in line with Linda Putnam's (1983) claim that we face two competing perspectives within the society of science. Functionalistic theory, understood as a global category of a broad range of positivist schools, is presented as having achieved a hegemonic status. Its counterpart is the interpretive perspective, with a focus on the subjective, intersubjective, and socially constructed meaning of the actors. These two perspectives are in a sort of conceptual bondage where the interpretive approach may be understood in a historical perspective as a reaction against the dominant position of the functionalistic perspective in general and the use of functionalistic theory on social phenomena in particular. Argyris et al. (1985) portrayed it as a split between a mainstream and a counterview of science, where the important distinction lies in the role of interpretation and creation of meaning.

Ghoshal, Mintzberg, and Czarniawska seemed to share a commitment to such an interpretive counterview, and a profound skepticism toward mainstream organizational science. I agree with these fine scholars' skepticism when it comes to the hegemony of functionalistic organization theory. I also find the dominance of the eye of science in organization theory to be devastating, and I agree that management education that builds on one-eyed management is dangerous. But I am more reluctant when it comes to a general condemnation of functionalistic theories and management science. As I see it (and I believe I am in line with Cassirer here), the eye of science—whether we name it functionalistic, positivistic, modernistic, empiricist, rational, or analytic—has a specific relevance in organization theory. It is true that these theories, as Putnam (1993) indicates, view social phenomena as concrete and materialistic, as different kinds of social facts. Accordingly, social life, norms, values, and roles tend to become hard and accurate statistic facts; and social reality becomes something that exists separately from individuals. It is also true that some interpretive theories regard reality as socially constructed. An organization with its norms, roles, routines, plans, charts, emotions, and values becomes a result of actors' ongoing efforts to create meaning in social actions.

I also agree that interpretive theories' depiction of organizations seems closer to organizational reality as it unfolds and thus is more realistic than functionalistic theories. However, if we deprive managers of the ability to reduce complexity by means of elaborate methods, we also deprive them of the important capacity to direct attention to, separate, and make sense of floating sensuous phenomena in a highly effective manner, according to Cassirer. Without this capacity, managers are left with a stream of sensuous impressions from which it is difficult to derive explanations, finalities, and causalities. Consequently, the capacity to reflect and learn is reduced, as is the ability to predict possible future outcomes of present actions.

THE NEED FOR RECONCILIATION

Both Nonaka (1991) and Wheatley (1992) claimed that the roots of the functionalistic tradition within organization theory are to be found in the expansion and dominance of the natural sciences. The attained hegemonic position of the natural sciences thus led to what is often regarded as a machine view of organizations:

> The machine imagery of the spheres was captured by organizations in an emphasis on structure and parts. Responsibility has been organized into functions. People have been organized into roles. Page after page of organizational charts depict the workings of the machine: the number of pieces, what fits where, who the big pieces are.
>
> (Wheatley 1992: 27)

Organizations are seen as machines, fixed structures, and neutral bureaucracies. The focus is primarily on concrete surface phenomena, formal plans, quantitative goals and objectives, and hierarchical organizational structures. Management becomes a rational process of prediction, programming, and control; and organizational change becomes something to be controlled and managed by means of formal planning and quantifiable goals. Knowledge is a commodity or a "thing" in a concrete world that can be revealed through the use of systematic methods and quantitative techniques (Newell, Robertson, Scarbrough, and Swan 2002).

Treating organizations as if they were machines is obviously a cruel simplification. But it is not necessarily erroneous; and it may even be productive. Most organizations have at least some machine-like features, sometimes to such a large degree that the picture of the organization as a machine becomes the most accurate metaphor. Simplification through routines and standardization is also required if we as consumers are to have access to inexpensive products; it is required if quality is to be ensured; and it is often considered necessary if knowledge from previous learning is to become organizational and not just individual.

Organizations seem to have a drive towards simplification and towards production in a "rational mode," according to Bill Torbert (1989). He is in line with Charles Perrow, who claimed that routinization, standardization, and bureaucracy appear to be inherent in the nature of an industrial civilization (Perrow 1970: 179). One of the reasons is that organizations try to minimize the impact of extra-organizational influences upon members and to control, as much as possible, the uncertainties and variabilities of the environment, Perrow held forth. Trying to simplify organizations is thus intelligent and not a result of " . . . nervous, insecure, petty officials bent on protecting the status quo at all odds or on maximizing their individual power" (Perrow 1970: 178).

But Perrow also made a case for transcending the technology of administration and emphasizing institutional elements such as organizational mission and character and the responsiveness of what he called the inevitably bureaucratic, authoritarian organization to a presumably democratic society. Perrow claimed that the solution is not to try to do away with structure and routines (i.e., to eliminate bureaucracy), but to make the difference bigger. In line with the classical study of Lawrence and Lorsch (1967), he maintained that some parts of an organization are, and should be, more routine-based than others; thus, these parts call for standardized methods and mechanistic ways of organizing. Donald Schön (1983) argued along the same lines: He maintained that different "zones of practice" exist in an organization, some more unique than others. In the unique zones of practice, people have the opportunity to place their personal "fingerprints" on their work, so they have at least a certain degree of choice when it comes to deciding how a job is to be performed. These unique zones call for on-the-spot solutions and improvisation.

According to institutional theory, the personal ways of conducting work may lead to an institutionalization process by which norms and values are infused into the organization (Selznick 1957). Such is not the case in the repetitive zones of practice, at least not to the same degree. The more mechanistic and repetitive an organization is, the less the possibility that an institutional process may lead to the development of deep organizational levels of ideologies, values, and norms. Consequently, managers need to see how organizations differ, and they need the practical knowledge that makes them capable of handling different zones of practice in productive ways. Nonunique zones are characterized by repetitiveness. They represent continuity more than change; the context is to a large degree controllable; and it is possible to predict what is going to happen with a larger degree of certainty. Applying functionalistic approaches with a focus on concrete surface phenomena and linear relationships under these machine-like conditions may then be the best choice. This approach is, however, obviously not unproblematic. As we have already seen, several problems are involved in the transfer of scientific approaches from the natural sciences to the social sciences (Elster 1983), particularly regarding the use of explanations and the meaning of actors' intentions. Thus, treating social systems as if they were physical or biological systems is undoubtedly questionable. Functional explanations cannot straightforwardly be applied to social systems.[5] However, organizations sometimes resemble physical systems. Breweries are an example. Most breweries today have gone through technological revolutions, and production is now completely automated and computerized. As a whole, a brewery today rather resembles a mechanistic than a social system.

In other words, certain conditions make functional theory applicable for the study of intra-organizational processes.[6] The functionalistic tradition stems from early natural science research where the context was characterized by a large degree of prediction and control, such as when Galileo Galilei turned his telescope towards lunar craters and the moons revolving around Jupiter. Cause-and-effect relationships between phenomena with a rather unproblematic, at least physical, ontological status were in focus. The relationship between the subject (e.g., the researcher) and the object (e.g., what was studied) as well as the context in which the research took place was often controlled. The same contextual characteristics apply to many nonunique zones of practice in organizations, where the work is carried out based on repetitive patterns and the control with the environment is tight. In other words, applying functionalistic theories that in essence treat organizations as if they were simplified into machines might be, under the right conditions, a good alternative. However, if functionalistic theories are applied unreflectively under the wrong conditions (such as when the context is characterized by a large degree of uncertainty, discontinuity, and flux) and the work is carried out based on personal skills more than pre-given routines, more problems will probably be produced than solved.

It has often been said that organizations today exist in uncertain and unpredictable contexts where formal planning and forecasting must be replaced by improvisation and exploration (e.g., Brown and Eisenhardt 1997; Hatch 1999; Kamoche and Cunha 2001; Montuori 2003; Moorman and Miner 1998; Orlikowski 1996, Senge 1990; Tsoukas and Chia 2002). But at the same time many organizations must increasingly strive towards standardized modes of production in order to survive. Robotization, automatization, and fine-tuned logistics become fundamental for their survival in a competitive world. That is, mechanistic and organistic zones of practice coexist and cannot be managed productively by applying the same "eye" in every situation. Treating organizations as if they were machines will most likely create dysfunctional effects if the context is characterized by dynamic complexity and uncertainty, and the organization is highly institutionalized and infused with values. Also, it is unproductive to treat organizations and zones of practice as if they were complex networks of emerging patterns, governed by emotions and deep-level ideologies, when they are actually closer to simple machines.

Clearly, the need exists for approaches that are simple and mechanistic, as well as interpretive, organic, and artistic. A challenge for management learning is then to develop a systematic understanding of how zones of practice vary and how they interrelate, and how a combined functionalistic-interpretive or structural-cultural approach can be applied according to the situation at hand. In daily work, the zones of practice are often deeply interwoven. Many tasks and processes are a mix of interrelated unique and repetitive practice zones, performed in organizational contexts consisting of both surface and deep organizational levels. Both mechanistic and organic processes then take place simultaneously. Accordingly, a need exists for practical knowledge that can illuminate at the same time both zones and the interrelationship between deep and surface layers. These forms of knowledge are found on each side of the main divide in organizational theory. Today's situation, I think, calls for a combination of these types of knowledge, which implies a need for bringing together antagonistic traditions of organization theory in order to establish a new dialogue.

ON THE CHALLENGE OF DEVELOPING TWO-EYED CURRICULA: THE MKL CASE

In 2002, my university college asked me to develop a curriculum for a new part-time master's program. The result was the 90 ECTS[7] Master of Knowledge Management program (MKL). It has run every year since the first class was enrolled in 2003. MKL has been considered a success. The classes are filled every year, and the advertisement costs are low. Also, the student results have been good when measured through exams and the master thesis. However, the narratives of success hide tension and conflicts that may tell us something about the challenges of developing a "two-eyed" curriculum. I will first sketch the curriculum, and thereafter discuss some of the challenges I experienced when attempting to put the plan's espoused theories into action.[8]

The Study Plan's Espoused Theory of Action

The study plan stated that we are living in a knowledge society. In the Western world, the level of education is higher than ever before. Accordingly, managers often have to lead people who know more than the managers themselves do. This situation by itself poses serious challenges to managers. Knowledge becomes a competitive edge, not only for profit organizations, but also for the public sector, including local governments. Knowledge and creativity become pivotal to an organization's capacity to innovate and change. New technology changes the rules of the game, and one of the consequences is that managers have to lead people they seldom meet face to face. Many companies tear down their pyramids and establish flat organizational forms. Networks replace formal bureaucratic organizations.

All in all, the study plan said that old ways of managing people and long-established traditions must be questioned in a knowledge society. Old solutions are not necessarily solutions to tomorrow's problems. Managers and change agents in the new knowledge society need competence that can help them navigate in this new complex landscape. The fact that they need to become reflective practitioners is, according to the study plan, why we developed MKL. Enrolling in MKL provides students the capacity to reflect critically upon organizational problems and solutions, so that they will become better at coping with and managing change, and they will learn how to develop organizations for a society in which situations often cannot be standardized or routinized.

The study plan also stated that MKL's perspective is systemic, relational, and social-constructive, where multiparadigmatic knowledge from such fields as music, pedagogy, literature, and drama may be helpful supplements to organizational theory.

The Structure of the Program

The program was designed as three parts, 30 ECTS each. The first part was Organizational Theory and Organized Practice; the second was Knowledge Management and Innovation; and the last involved the writing of a master's thesis. Parts 1 and 2 were divided into four modules each. After each module, the students were expected to write a five- to seven-page essay applying theory from the last module. There was also a one-week exam after both Part 1 and Part 2. Below is a short and far-from-complete sketch of the modules:

Module 1, Organizational Theory and Organized Practice, focused on the main historical traditions in organizational theory. Some of their consequences for today's business world were discussed, as well as the diversity of related theories. Module 2, Methodology, drew upon the lines from the main schools in the philosophy of science to different ways of studying organizations. The students were expected to become researchers in their own organizations. The emphasis was on how to develop actionable and useful knowledge for improving organizations.

Module 3, Organizational Development and Planned Change, addressed ways to become a change agent. Organizational learning, action theory, defensive routines, organizational culture, productive communication, organizational development, and the perils of planned change were the main subjects. Module 4, Strategy and Strategic Leadership, addressed different perspectives on strategy, models for strategic analysis and planning, strategic change processes, strategy implementation, and strategic leadership.

After a one-week exam covering the first four modules, Part 2 started with Module 5, Intellectual Capital and Knowledge Management. The agenda included the knowledge society, perspectives on knowledge in classic and contemporary theory, knowledge-intensive organizations, knowledge-sharing and knowledge-storing, and how to manage knowledge workers. Module 6, Knowledge and Methodology, returned to methodology and covered such topics as action research, action learning, and actionable knowledge. Module 7, Knowledge and Technology, concentrated on technology, humans and organization, new forms of technology, and how technology changes our workplaces. Module 8, Innovation and Creativity, addressed how to lead creative and innovative processes, improvisation and play, imagination, art, and aesthetics. After a one-week exam covering all four modules of Part 2, the students concentrated on writing their theses.

Although a Norwegian program taught in Norwegian, MKL for several reasons was developed as a joint degree in cooperation with Copenhagen Business School and Learning Lab Denmark (now a part of Aarhus University). The Norwegian faculty was in charge of Parts 1 and 2, whereas the Danes were formally in charge of Part 3. The students had to defend their master's theses in Copenhagen. One reason for the collaboration was that the college already had a successful Master in Public Administration program running together with the Danes.

Tensions and Challenges

Although the educational profile (e.g., teaching methods) and ideology were quite clearly expressed in the study plan, advertisements, and other program documents, different expectations existed among the students in the first two or three MKL classes in particular. Some students had read the study descriptions carefully and accepted that they would not be presented take-away solutions wrapped in inspirational lectures. But others reacted with annoyance, some with explicit anger. In the first classes, the academic level of the students was high, in the sense that all of them had already earned about 60 ECTS credits in organizational theory or topics related to management studies as part of or in addition to their professional education or BA. Many even had master's degrees before enrolling in MKL; in fact, two held PhDs.

In classroom discussions, it quickly became clear that the frustration they expressed at least to some degree was related to a feeling of having their prior education devaluated by the MKL faculty. Many were trained in mainstream management and functionalistic thinking. Some said the time spent on reflection in the classroom was a waste of time. They expected content delivery from the teachers; and they wanted solutions, models, and prescriptions.

Typically, the classes were divided into three camps: the structure and content camp, the process and reflection camp, and the in-betweens who asked for a bit of both. This picture seems, to a variable degree, to have characterized all the MKL classes since the first 2003 class. However, in the last few years' classes, the expectations of deliverance of structured solutions and simple models seem to have decreased, although the polarization between those who expect traditional lectures and content delivery (also in the form of delivery of anarchistic and unorthodox theories) and those who expect process learning seems to have continued. The result was tension between students, tension between students and teachers, and numerous class discussions about which learning methods are best. It also became evident that students favored different teachers. The process and reflection camp preferred teachers who were playful and creative, who employed art-based techniques, and who put less emphasis on traditional teacher-to-student knowledge transfer. The structure and content camp preferred teachers who gave lectures and then facilitated structured group work with theory-related questions. However, as the exams and the writing of the thesis neared, the process and reflection camp tended to become quieter. Discussions about learning methods became fewer, and the students' focus was increasingly on theory, writing skills, and academic topics they found relevant to exams and theses.

A second type of tension was induced independently of students by faculty and administration members. As mentioned earlier, the college already had a master's program running in Public Administration, the MPA program. MKL soon became part of the same governing structure as the MPA program. The MPA was a 120-ECTS part-time program, but was run in only two and a half years, whereas MKL as a 90 ECTS program took three years. According to faculty who taught in both programs, the MPA placed a heavier weight on structure theories, economics, and administration, and it problematized to a lesser degree the dilemmas inhibited in mainstream organizational theories.

Expectations of standardizing elements and modules in the MKL and MPA programs were soon voiced. Some modules, particularly the two methodology modules, were said to be so similar that the student classes should be merged. Teaching 70 to 80 students instead of half that number would reduce costs without lowering quality, it was said. Also, some claimed that MKL should not take longer than the MPA, that MKL should also be a 120-ECTS program, that the name should be altered from Master of Knowledge Management to Master of Knowledge Management and Innovation, and that MKL should be included in the partnership with the second Norwegian college of which the MPA was a part. Ultimately, MKL was included in the partnership with the second college, and fifty percent of the teachers were supposed to come from this college. Additionally, the name of the program was changed.

Lessons Learned

As should be clear from the module descriptions, MKL was not developed as a blueprint for a "two-eyed" curriculum. Nevertheless, a thread that runs through all the modules as described in the study plan is the problems entailed in applying "wrong" theories in organizational contexts, and the reflective capacity to "see" organizations differently, according to the context at hand. The curriculum problematized strong beliefs in formal plans, hierarchical organizational structures, prediction, programming, and control that were engrained in some of the students from prior studies; but it also problematized the naïve and romantic conception of management as being power-independent processes of interpretations, feelings, values, and the construction of mental images. It emphasized the development of a reflective capacity in the students that could help them distinguish between functional and dysfunctional management theories and organizational processes. It did not debunk structured methods and functional theory; rather, it problematized the usefulness of these theories and bureaucratic theories in contexts characterized by uncertainty and complexity.

I think it is fair to say that the curriculum tried to include the eye of science as well as the eye of art, but that we as a faculty seldom succeeded in illustrating how the two eyes interacted and how their different strengths could be harnessed to create extraordinary results. Instead, the polarization among the students when it came to expectations of lectures that presented models and solutions versus expectations of process learning that employed art-based techniques, also seemed to lead to a polarity among teachers. Theoretical content as well as teaching methods became, to a large degree, colored by the faculty who was in charge of the particular module, independently of what the study plan said about teaching methods. For example, in Module 8, if teachers from the art-based camp were in charge, the emphasis was on art and aesthetics instead of how to manage innovative projects. In contrast, when teachers from the content delivery camp lectured, the emphasis was on how to plan and structure innovative projects, with fewer examples from art and fewer creative and artistic processes.

In other words, faculty by themselves decided how the MKL curriculum as an espoused theory was taken into theories-in-use in the classroom. Still, the power of a student group made up of 40- to 60-year-old managers and would-be managers should not be underestimated. In a typical class, some students had all their costs covered by their employers; some had to pay part or all of the cost themselves; and some were running their own companies and were very aware of the fact that they lost money each hour they spent in a class that they found to be a waste of time. And all of them seemed to have one thing in common: at work, no one was doing their job while they were at school. So most of them had high expectations when it came to what the teachers should present to them, which probably would have been easier to handle from a faculty point of view if MKL did not have two-eyed ambitions. Following a knowledge-transfer paradigm, tension is reduced through detailed curricula and tightly planned teaching. Following a process-based learning paradigm, responsibility is shared and learning takes place as collective reflection and inquiry facilitated by faculty (Irgens and Ertsas 2008; Nygaard and Holtham 2008). The students soon identified some of the teachers as belonging to either the knowledge-transfer or the process-based learning paradigm. Because a class, at least in the first part of the program when exams and thesis still seemed to be far away, typically was polarized in two antagonistic camps, a teacher would usually get positive feedback from at least one student group. I suspect that this feedback contributed to a polarization among faculty. Faculty in general chose to teach the way they were used to teaching in other programs: they stuck to their teaching paradigms. I did notice some exceptions: in some modules, although sufficient resources were lacking, teachers chose to teach in pairs. This often led to a spread of alternative teaching methods and creative techniques.

What were my lessons learned? First, a curriculum that is multiparadigmatic and draws on plural forms of knowledge is indeed challenging to both students and faculty (in my opinion, to faculty in particular). Already designed into the curriculum were tension between functionalistic and interpretive approaches, between structure and process theories, between management science and art, and between content delivery and process learning, to name a few. Such tensions tend to surface in the meeting between faculty and students. Tension is an inevitable part of learning (Illeris 2002); in theory, they should be welcomed or at least harnessed as opportunities for learning in the classroom (Irgens and Ertsas 2008). Turning the class into a learning organization should accordingly be a formula for accelerated learning, because many processes that take place in a classroom involving adult students and faculty resemble what the students experience in their workplaces. We have students who strongly voice their learning ideology and try to move the class in the direction they are convinced is the best; we have students who remain silent; we see anxiety and defensive routines in play; and conflicts surface and must be addressed in one way or another.

All are potential learning situations that can be used to illustrate theory, as well as to reflect collectively upon what is going on in actual work organizations. They can be used as learning situations if the faculty (a) allows it and (b) has the capacity to lead and participate in these learning processes. Such a situation requires the capacity to improvise in the classroom when unpredicted situations surface. However, whereas some faculty members design their teaching in ways that allow processes to emerge and improvisation to take place, others do not. Improvisation succeeds best when optimal flexibility is permitted within minimal structures (Barrett and Peplowski 1998). The structure should not lock up the inquiry process, but should serve as a starting point and a reference base. Even jazz is built on structure (Alterhaug 2004), but it is not structured to the degree that improvisation is not allowed to take place. However, some teachers communicate to the class that they have much content to cover; they lecture according to a sequential plan; and when they allow process, it is typically in the form of a structured group assignment related to the theories the teacher has covered. Tension and here-and-now learning situations seldom surface when these faculty members lecture; and if they do, they are seldom harnessed as opportunities for here-and-now learning. That does not mean the tension is removed: in a class that meets regularly, tension that is not allowed to surface will sooner or later find new ways to come up. And one obvious place for this tension to surface is the classes conducted by process/creative faculty members, because these classes provide a better opportunity for discussion. Thus, the burden is left to the process/creative teachers to handle, and in turn polarization among faculty may increase.

Institutional effects are also in play. I call them institutional because they either are results of experiences in prior institutional contexts that are reproduced in the new context, or they are already inhibited in the new institutional setting. First, what students have learned from prior studies shapes their expectations of the class and of the faculty. For example, some students expect faculty to be democratic and allow students to have a say, whereas others believe that they should not "waste time on endless processes and discussions." For MKL, the strongest institutional effect was probably the power of exams: even the most process-loving students became silent and appreciated content delivery when the exams were approaching. As long as students are evaluated on written exams and theses alone, it is difficult to steer clear of this effect. A third institutional effect came from faculty members themselves, as we experienced attempts to fuse MKL and MPA classes in methodology. The rationale was that "methodology is methodology," and the only difference was between qualitative and quantitative methods, which nevertheless should be taught in both classes.

A curriculum will always be based on an ideology, explicit or not. The ideal situation when developing a "two-eyed" curriculum would be a devoted faculty who are committed to the chosen ideology, who are trained in using the eye of science as well as the eye of art, and who have the willingness and capacity to make the curriculum's intentions come alive in the classroom. This may be wishful thinking. Therefore, a more realistic solution would be to have a core faculty in addition to faculty members who are more peripheral to the chosen ideology. The role of the core faculty group would then be to assure that continual reflection occurs throughout the whole program, to take responsibility for the processes that are needed in order to handle tensions, and to make sure the pedagogical and ideological thread that has to run through the whole program in order to avoid fragmentation is never lost. I am convinced that without a devoted core faculty, any attempt to develop two-eyed management programs is a waste of time.

7 The Institution as a Symbolic Form

In this last chapter, I discuss if we can regard the modern institution as a symbolic form and, if so, what we can gain from assigning such a role. I show how bureaucratic logics have become a metastandard for organizing, and how this metastandard molds the way we experience and behave, not only in, but also outside institutions. Seeing the institution as a symbolic form may help us (a) see the strengths and the weaknesses of institutions' specific levels of refraction and particular logics, (b) see how different symbolic forms coexist and influence behavior in organizations and how we may gain a better and more realistic picture of organizations if we become proficient in understanding organizations through different forms, and (c) develop curricula that are more realistic. I close the chapter by discussing how pluralism may lead to unity and the need for bringing the best of the humanities into management education.

COUNTER-HISTORICAL SPECULATIONS

As I began writing this final chapter, I thought of Ludwig Wittgenstein, who, in the introduction to his Tractatus Logico-Philosophicus (published in German in 1921, in English in 1922), said that its purpose would be achieved if it gave pleasure to one person who understood it.

That is indeed modest! Or perhaps just arrogant? The latter is likely because Wittgenstein thought he had solved all philosophical problems in his book. In his introduction, he also said that his book perhaps would be understood by only someone who had already had the same thoughts, or at least similar thoughts, that were expressed in it. I wonder if Wittgenstein was a strategist as well. Maybe he, just like me, was afraid of what the critics would say, and merely tried in his introduction to take some of the sting out.

Reflecting upon my piece of writing (which clearly has little to do with Wittgenstein), I realize that it will be attacked from both flanks, from positivists as well as radical social constructivists. I have not found a place to seek shelter. And that is illustrative, I think, when it comes to understanding the task of this book. It can be criticized for not really contributing anything new, for having misinterpreted Cassirer (as well as Heidegger, radicalism, analytic philosophy, positivism, and constructivism), for not acknowledging important schools (e.g., semantic analysis, semiotics, actor-network theory, complexity theory, theory on leaders as artists), for leaving out contributions to develop integrated views,[1] for wasting time and energy on a lost cause, for not providing the answers, and for not posing the right questions.

I struggle to find shelter! It may sound like self-pity, and it may seem like I am asking for sympathy. What I am trying to say is merely that there are few communities within management education and organization theory that are absorbed in the same ideas. I seek a place where I find my organizational theory allies, where I can get the intellectual ammunition I need, where new energy and resources are to be found. I cannot without difficulty identify a school within organizational theory that is truly committed to the types of discussions and investigations that Cassirer represented. So when I am criticized, my first response will be a reminder that we have lost more than 75 years since the dialogue ended, and that is a long time. We certainly have much work to do. There are so many questions to be asked and so many answers to be found, and if this book had provided the answers, it would have been a contribution towards closure instead of an invitation to open dialogue.

The division seems to have grown since the science war of the 1990s. In a counter-historical perspective, it is interesting to try to picture how philosophy in general and organizational theory in particular would have developed *if* Cassirer had not been forced to depart Europe, leaving continental Europe open for Heidegger to dominate (Friedman 2000, 2002, 2005). I am pretty sure that we today would still have had the two main positions. But I also think that the middle Cassirerian position would have been stronger, and that cross-paradigmatic debates would have taken place more frequently. Maybe we even would have had more management education programs emphasizing multiple ways of knowing, combining, and harnessing the eye of science as well as the eye of art.

I admit that I may sound naïve. And I also admit that it is easy to become carried away when studying Cassirer, and that this book really should have had a more critical distance from his theory. Cassirer may indeed be very seducing. The counter-historical perspective alone is fascinating. Cassirer's analysis of brain-impaired patients long before neuroscience had access to brain scanning methods is captivating. The way he takes his own medicine, in the sense that he draws on allegories and examples from various parts of man's cultural life, makes his works tremendously rich. And his writing style, where poetic language and logical-rational reasoning meet, just makes the seducing power even stronger.[2]

STUDENTS' QUEST FOR REALISTIC KNOWLEDGE

Among the many good reasons for studying Cassirer, I find most compelling his promise that I will turn into a better practitioner if I become capable of applying different symbolic forms. Thus, it is indeed a philosophy of hope that he presented. The attractiveness of Cassirer's theory becomes particularly strong in light of the challenges that management training and education are facing. Many demarcation lines can be identified in the ongoing debates in management education. One of the most evident seems to be, as I have tried to show in this book, between what Putnam (1983) labeled functionalistic and interpretive perspectives, the first with roots in analytic philosophy, the latter in a hermeneutic and constructivist tradition. In my own practice as a management educator, I have experienced various responses from students to theories from the two sides. I have, for example, found teaching younger and inexperienced students theories related to management science rather unproblematic. The curricula have been concrete and not blurred by attempts to draw on and to problematize plural forms of knowledge, the models easy to teach in accordance with a traditional knowledge transfer tradition, and the content well-suited for traditional exams. On the other hand, experienced students—as long as they have been motivated to become better practitioners rather than to survive an academic exam—have often rejected both the models and the way of learning through content transfer from teacher to student.

However, teaching the same experienced students organizational theory in the radical constructivist tradition—where organizations, including processes, people, and physical objects, are cognitively and socially constructed—has not been heartily welcomed either. Many of the experienced managers I have met throughout the years have decided to study part-time because they sincerely wanted to improve their own practice and organizations, or what they regarded as their own *reality*. This type of student soon finds it uninteresting and unmotivating to spend time on theories that seem to deny them access to the real world they want to improve. This is, of course, a simplified way of depicting the situation, but it touches the core of a problem that I have often faced when teaching and training practitioners. To learn about narrative techniques in order to analyze what is going on, as well as to learn about how narratives work within organizations, is usually seen as helpful. However, if narratives are all there is, all we can access, or if narratives and texts somewhat cover the real world and protect it from intervention, many of my practitioners sooner or later seem to lose interest.

As an example of a "soft" constructivist theory, "enacted sense-making" (Morgan 1986, 1991; Weick 1979, 1982) has met mixed interest by my practitioners.

If we shift to a more self-conscious efferent imagery and if we blur the boundaries between organizations and environments, and if we selectively use open systems imagery, then we put ourselves in a better position to say that a substantial number of the enacted environments associated with organizations consist of personal ideas that are extended outward, implanted, and rediscovered.

(Weick 1982: 290)

The idea that the world (in Weick's words, "a substantial number of the enacted environments") is enacted through processes of outward extension has to some degree been accepted by my students, but the expectation of "something more" has been strong. "Weick does not give us the whole picture" has been a typical response. To offer a richer picture, they have sometimes given their own accounts of busy environments where they, in line with Weick, extended their ideas outward, but also continually and aggressively were bombarded by the ideas of others, as well as by processes and technology and what they regard as a "very real and objective world." They tell me that they often feel vulnerable. Many deny that much of what they are "fighting with" is their own rediscovered ideas, as Weick claimed. They report that they are struggling with far more than their own ideas extended outwards, and they often do not have a protective shield strong enough to create a filter or disconnection between themselves and the world around them. Reality is difficult. They are challenged by more than their own ideas; in fact, they assert that their own ideas are just a small portion of the whole.

They do not completely reject Weick's description; they simply claim that it is not a sufficiently rich picture, and thus it is not what they are seeking when they are motivated to become better practitioners. It is not useful and realistic enough. This has become particularly evident to me when I have taught strategy. My students have seldom been motivated by being told that working with strategies is merely to play with one's own ideas that are extended outwards and rediscovered. It seems to be a piece of theory that, if taken literally, is denying them access to the real world, and thus represents a pessimistic view on the possibility of changing for the better.

Weick's (1995) renowned anecdote of the maps and the soldiers has brought up many discussions in my classes. As the story goes, after two days of heavy snow, the soldiers considered themselves lost and waited for the end. However, one of them found a map in his pocket, and they navigated safely back to the headquarters. It turned out that the map in fact was not a map of the Alps, but a map of the Pyrenees. I have asked my experienced students how they interpret the story, and what message they think Weick was trying to convey. "He tries to tell us that it does not matter if our plans are correct or not," has been a typical response. "It is more important to have a plan and to believe in it."

At this stage, the students usually come up with their own examples of the importance of good plans; of how lives have been saved, thanks to thoughtful and detailed planning; of how investments in expensive planning systems have revolutionized the company's efficiency and at the same time reduced costs; and of how "wrong" plans have led to near catastrophes. "It is actually the opposite of what Weick attempts to tell us. Without good, reliable, flexible, and realistic plans, we would have been out of business long ago." And these plans are not necessarily made by the managers themselves; they often come from, for example, planning departments, supervisors, or the board.

My use of Weick as an example is debatable. Weick, as I read him, is not a radical constructivist, and he does not claim that all of our enacted environments are personal ideas that are extended outward, implanted, and rediscovered. But he does claim that a substantial number are. At this point, most of my students disagree, although they might have different opinions about what a "substantial number" is. They point out that Weick's depiction of their work is not rich and close enough to be recognized as realistic, and to be seen as a valid point of departure for learning. As one of them said, "If that is all, what shall we do? What can you possibly teach us? Why are we here?"

A closer look at what my students say reveals that some of their reactions are based on first-hand experiences that have taught them that organizations affect how they think and act. These experiences are also emotional and bodily: they are lived experiences. They have become a part of the students themselves, influencing the way they interpret organizational effects and make managerial decisions. The students tell us that some of the ideas—in fact, most of them—with which they have to cope are not their own recycled or reinvented ideas that they once extended outwards and now rediscover. They tell us instead about effects that are actor-independent. There are effects and structures that are "objective" in organizations, something is "real," independent of their interpretations.

This brings us back to symbolic forms. Through symbolic forms, man constructs a shared and objective reality that goes beyond the particular here-and-now situation (Hoel 2006). Making sense of here-and-now experiences necessitates access to objective knowledge that already *is*. Symbolic forms are examples of culturally and historically developed and shared knowledge that already is. If we want to transcend our here-and-now situation and if we want to develop the capacity to change and improve our world, we must have objective knowledge. The symbolic forms as objective knowledge mold our experiences, parallel to how the organizations influenced my management students.

As far as I know, Cassirer never discussed organizations when he introduced his theory of symbolic forms. However, he often linked the cultural and historical development of symbolic forms to the organizing of human societies. Thus, the question that naturally arises is whether we can regard the modern institution as a symbolic form. If we can, we must consider what it takes, and what we can gain from assigning the institution such a role. I am very aware that this is a risky task, too big for a few pages, so I do not mean to give profound answers. My intention is merely to open the topic up for a debate.

AN ORGANIZATION AS A SYMBOLIC UNIVERSE

Biologist Jacob von Uexküll's theory of anatomic structures was pivotal in Cassirer's exploration of man as *animal symbolicum*. According to von Uexküll, all organisms are fitted into their environment, thanks to a receptor system, through which the organism receives outward stimuli, and an effector system, through which it reacts to the stimuli. The two systems are highly interwoven links in a chain that von Uexküll called a functional circle (*EoM*: 24).

Cassirer added a third system, the symbolic system, that he claimed was specific to man. The symbolic system, which has qualities other than those of the receptor end effector systems of lower animals, allows us not only to react but also to respond. The profound difference between man and other animals is the difference between organic reactions and human responses. The organic reaction involves a direct and immediate answer, whereas the human response involves a delay, during which a process of thought takes place. Man cannot escape his destiny: he lives not only in a physical universe, but also in a symbolic universe. Symbolic forms such as science, myth, art, and religion are parts of this universe: "They are the varied threads which weave the symbolic net, the tangled web of human experience" (*EoM*: 25). Man is unable to confront reality immediately. If man's symbolic activity advances, the physical reality seems to move away:

> Instead of dealing with the things themselves man is in a sense constantly conversing with himself. He has so enveloped himself in linguistic forms, in artistic images, in mythical symbols or religious rites that he cannot see or know anything except by the interposition of this artificial medium. His situation is the same in the theoretical as in the practical sphere. Even here man does not live in a world of hard facts, or according to his immediate needs and desires. He lives rather in the midst of imaginary emotions, in hopes and fears, in illusions and disillusions, in his fantasies and dreams.
>
> (*EoM*: 25)

Here we arrive at what seems to be Cassirer's main mission: to correct and enlarge the classical definition of man as an *animal rationale*. Rationality has occupied a too dominating role, he seems to argue. On the one hand, rationality is inherent in all activities of man, even in myth. On the other hand, even in logical and scientific language we find a primary language of poetic imagination that expresses feelings and affections, rather than thoughts of ideas. We are offered only *pars pro toto* (part of the whole), if we accept rationality's dominating role. Even rational theories are no more than abstractions, if we follow Cassirer.

> Reason is a very inadequate term with which to comprehend the forms of man's cultural life in all their richness and variety. . . . Hence, instead of defining man as an *animal rationale,* we should define him as an *animal symbolicum.* By so doing we can designate his specific difference, and we can understand the new way open to man—the way to civilization.
>
> (*EoM*: 26)

In the destiny of man—to be doomed to live in a symbolic world—also lies the hope of man, the path to freedom. Symbolic knowledge is a key to higher forms of consciousness and to the development of societies, including work organizations. Symbolic knowledge offers us the opportunity to reflect, to prioritize based on values and standards—in short, to respond and not merely to react.

ORGANIZATIONS AS ABSTRACT AND SYMBOLIC SPACE

Jacob von Uexküll's theory of the functional circle as an anatomic structure that makes every living being capable of fitting into its environment has obvious parallels in the system-oriented organizational theories that surfaced in the 1950s and early 1960s. Through the receptor system, the organization receives outward stimuli; and through the effector system, it reacts to the stimuli. Cassirer proposed the symbolic system, to be found somewhere between the receptor and effector systems, as the distinctive mark of man and the historical development of civilization.

Civilization is the manifestation of man's attempt to organize his social life. A formal organization is likewise an expression of man's sophisticated attempts to organize work activities. Modern organizations have "elaborated" ears, such as market departments that scan the environment for changes in trends and preferences; from this and other receptor systems, consequences are derived that result in new or adjusted outputs from the effector system. These responses are, according to Cassirer, not mechanistic or biological, but mediated through the organization's symbolic system where the responses are molded through symbolic forms. We do find inclinations of symbolic activities in higher animals, but the intelligence and imagination are of a different type. "In short we may say that animal processes a practical imagination and intelligence whereas man alone has developed a new form: a symbolic imagination and intelligence" (*EoM*: 33).

The rise of the formal work organization is a remarkable example of man's ability to organize his life symbolically. Man organizes his world in space and time, according to Cassirer. The significance of space and time cannot be fully understood through psychological methods alone. We must analyze the forms of culture to understand their meanings in our human world.

Organizing is not only a question of organizing work activities, but also of organizing space and time. According to Cassirer, we have different types of temporal and spatial experiences. We may talk of lower and higher strata as illustrated in Table 7.1: the lowest animals live in an *organic* space and time. Although these organisms' reactions may be complicated, they are immediate and not always learned through individual experience, as can be observed with newborn babies as well as newborn animals. At a higher level, we find animals that live in a more complex *perceptual* space. Here they draw upon elements of all sense experiences (tactual, optical, acoustic, and kinesthetic) in order to navigate in the environment. The line between humans and animals is found in *symbolic* space. Here we arrive at *abstract* space, a less physical space where we are concerned " . . . not with the truth of things but with the truth of propositions and definitions" (*EoM*: 44).

In the lower strata, the primitive spaces, we find few traces of abstract space. The action is centered on immediate needs and interests. It is an area of practical concerns and primitive conceptions without theoretical reflection.

Cassirer described man's development towards symbolic, abstract space as a historical and cultural development rather than a biological development of consciousness. As such, it is also a depiction of the social development of knowledge: it takes certain knowledge to navigate in abstract, symbolic space. This knowledge must be developed. Cassirer used the tribesman as an illustration: he may be an expert in navigating in concrete space, but when asked to handle abstract spatial relations he may find himself totally lost. "The native is perfectly acquainted with the course of the river, but this acquaintance is very far from what we may call knowledge in an abstract, a theoretical sense. Acquaintance means only presentation; knowledge includes and presupposes representation" (*EoM*: 46). This representation requires the ability to regard the object from different angles and to relate it to other objects in a larger system.

Table 7.1 Different Strata of Space Experiences

Strata:	Characteristics:
Symbolic space	Abstract space. Animal is inferior to man.
Perceptual space	Tactual, optical, acoustic, and kinesthetic orientation. Physical, concrete world.
Organic space	The space of action/direct reactions to environment. Man is inferior to animal.

In the lower strata, an organism may survive only by relying on well-developed receptor and effector systems. However, if such a thing as a symbolic system exists between a formal work organization's receptor system and its effector system, it follows that a good organization is inhibited by actors who have prolific knowledge of the abstract and symbolic space and the skills it takes to navigate in these higher-level strata: it is the actors who develop the symbolic system into an expression of their collective level of consciousness.

SYMBOLIC PREGNANCE IN AND FROM INSTITUTIONS

In order to understand how (and if) the institution can be regarded as symbolic forms, I find it helpful to draw on symbolic pregnance, a core concept in Cassirer's theory. This takes us back to neurobiology and the notion of the soma.

As we saw in Chapter 5, the neuroscientists claim to have proved that cognition and rational thinking take place against a background of emotions. Emotions are caused by certain situations that have led to bodily memory of how we felt when we experienced them. The bodily memory associated with the situation is called the soma.

Emotions are autonomous physiological reactions that occur in the limbic system as part of the interpretation of observations. These reactions take place before the observation is used in the rational frontal lobes. So the limbic system's autonomic reaction causes attention to shift to the stimuli that has caused an emotion. To be exact; the associated emotion causes the attention to shift (du Plessis 2005). This emotion can both intensify and change the direction of our attention, causing us to shun the situation at hand or to get closer, according to the somatic marker hypothesis (Bechara and Damasio 2005; Dalgleish 2004; Damasio et al. 1996).

We have already discussed some of the parallels and differences between the neuroscientists and Cassirer. We make sense of a situation through different interrelated processes, according to neuroscience; the first is intuitive and immediate, and the second is conscious and rational. The world is first given to us through immediate sensations, and then a classification process takes place and further structures our experiences (*PSF* 3: 129). Both the neurobiologist Damasio and the philosopher Cassirer claimed that these processes should be seen as one, and not as detached. Here we arrive at another parallel between neurobiology and the theory of symbolic forms: where the neuroscientists from their biological point of view introduce the soma, Cassirer from the perspective of culture brings in pregnance as a genuine a priori. "By symbolic pregnance we mean the way in which a perception as a sensory experience contains at the same time a certain non-intuitive meaning which it immediately and concretely represents" (*PSF* 3: 202).

Symbolic pregnance is a "transcendental element in Cassirer's philosophy of symbolic forms" and "the condition of the possibility of a consciousness and of symbolic forms of culture" (Krois in Paetzold 2002-1: 50). We are marked and shaped as human bodies by culture and the symbolic forms culture takes. These forms (e.g., myth, history, art, religion, language, and science) are dynamic forms that pass through phases throughout history. By the means of symbolic pregnance, they mold our sensory perceptions. Thus, we should expect Cassirer to be sympathetic to modern psychology, but that was not the case, with one exception: Cassirer was sympathetic to Gestalt psychology (*PSF* 1: 102). According to Gestalt psychology, our sense impressions are structured due to our fields of experience.

> Symbolic pregnance, then, is pointing to the fact that culture needs embodiment. Culture is mediated by human bodies. The agent of such an embodiment is what I would like to call a "cultured subjectivity." It is a potential everyone is acquainted with and, of course, introduced to by education. Education introduces individuals into the specificities of symbolic codings which belong to each culture in particular. Symbolic pregnance points to the fact that everyone has to start to go beyond his/her prestructurings by culture.
>
> (Paetzold 2002-1: 50–51)

How symbolic pregnance works is largely overlooked, according to Cassirer. Through the symbolic forms, pregnance is a precondition for all of man's experiences.[3] The forms have their distinctive ways of affecting us. The doctrine of symbolic pregnance is one of the most important theoretical topics in Cassirer's entire philosophy, according to Krois:

> According to this doctrine, there can be no such thing as uninterpreted phenomena, neither of the sort that Carnap called "Elementarerlebnisse"—momentary cross sections of a holistic empirical conception—nor Husserl's phenomenological conception of hyle, the "matter" of phenomenological reality. These are constructs that fail to recognize symbolic pregnance: that at no point are phenomena ever fully non-symbolic. That would be their annihilation. What philosophers—and not just philosophers—usually call "sensation" or "intuition" is really a symbolic phenomenon. The symbolic forms of culture are extensions of symbolic pregnance, which is found already in the *Leib-Seele* relation. (Krois 2009: 11)

Whereas human culture and the consciousness of man evolve, so does the number of symbolic forms, and Cassirer extended the examples of forms that he analyzed and also pointed to new forms. When he wrote *The Philosophy of Symbolic Forms* in the 1920s, he concentrated on myth, language, and science. However, in the second volume of *The*

Philosophy of Symbolic Forms, he also pointed to technology, law, ethics, and economics as possible symbolic forms. In the 1940s, when he wrote *An Essay on Man,* he added religion, history, and arts to the list of forms. It seems clear that Cassirer was open to several types of forms. Verene (1969) concluded that Cassirer regarded any area of culture as a potential symbolic form, depending on "(. . .) whether it can be shown to have a distinctive logical structure " (44). I would add that in order to be called a symbolic form, a distinctive logical structure is not enough. This specific area must also have gained a definite position in man's cultural life so that it can be said to be a representative expression of man's consciousness at a certain time in history, and that its logics more or less have become taken for granted within at least the specific area of social life where it is most dominant.

Should the modern institution then be regarded as a symbolic form? My answer, at least if I build my conclusion on institutional theory, is *yes.*[4] I have three main reasons for my conclusion. First, since Cassirer, we have seen a tremendous growth in institutions. According to Nancy Adler (2006), 49 of the 100 largest economies in the world are multinational companies, not countries. The world's largest private-sector company, Wal-Mart, has over 1.8 million employees worldwide, and more people in uniform than the U.S. Army, Adler tells us. Second, the political power of institutions has also increased immensely. Wal-Mart is the nineteenth largest economy in the world, according to Adler. If Wal-Mart were a country, Adler points out, it would be China's eighth-largest trading partner, in a position to do nearly whatever they may wish to. Third, not only have bureaucratic institutional logics (e.g., technical rationality, time management, and logistics) gained a dominant position within organizations; they have also invaded our lives. We have books that teach us how to run our family as if it was a company; we can buy computer-based time management systems that promise to help us get more out of our lives when we are off work; and management gurus publish management books for young people, teaching them how to develop logistics so that they can structure their lives better and become "highly effective."

Historically, formal work organizations have developed into symbolic forms, especially over the last 150 to 200 years. That is not to say that formal work organizations did not exist up to about 1800–1850; they obviously did. But several things changed. First, the number of formal organizations increased rapidly. Second, the formalization of the organizations intensified. Third, more organizations grew and reached a size that had never before been seen. Fourth, many organizations spread geographically. Clearly, organizations have become extremely powerful. We are born in institutions; we get our education in institutions; we marry and we divorce in institutions. We even die in institutions.

Position, number, and size are nonetheless not sufficient to qualify something as a symbolic form; it must also have the capacity to mold our sensory perceptions through symbolic pregnance (i.e., to influence the way we think and act in open as well as covert ways). For the institution to be a symbolic form, it must have the power to influence us in subtle ways. The most prominent theory that aims at explaining how organizations affect us when they turn into institutions is institutional theory. An important root of institutional theory goes back to Phillip Selznick (1957) and his work on institutionalization. Selznick theorized that an organization may change from being a rational, impersonal, goal-oriented formal system to an institution—a historically integrated and dynamic product infused with values. He claimed that the term "organization" makes us think of a rational, task-coordinating technical instrument aimed at reaching goals, whereas the term "institution" is an adaptable organism, a product of social needs and influences that can no longer be regarded as a neutral mechanism. It is a process of institutionalization that transcends the organization into a socially constituted institution with a distinct character. The distinction is analytic rather than descriptive, Selznick held forth. A corporation will always be a mix of the two forms, a complicated amalgam of the results of planning and the results of adaption; consequently, all forms of organization will have some degree of institutionalization.

Institutional theory has changed considerably since classic institutional theory was developed, but neo-institutional theory has maintained an emphasis on processes where rules, norms, schemas, and routines become authoritative guidelines that influence behavior (Borum and Westenholz 1995; Scott 1995; Tolbert and Zucker 1996). When organizations become institutions, they can no longer be seen as neutral structures and technical arrangements alone, but become infused with values, ideologies and logics. They start affecting actors in ways that are often hidden from the actors themselves through "silent" logics and taken-for-granted levels of refraction, parallel to Cassirer's depiction of the way symbolic forms influence us through pregnance.

Cassirer warned against habitual blindness as a result of subscribing to only one symbolic form. We also see habitual blindness developing when the taken-for-grantedness and subtle power of institutional logics make organizational members follow scripts and procedures without critical reflection or analysis of the situation at hand. Taken-for-granted logics secure rapid standard responses and create homogenous cultures. Both can be seen as productive from an efficiency perspective; however, these institutional processes may also be dangerous. Wicks' (2001) study of the 1992 explosion at Westray Mines is illustrative. Wicks concluded that a mindset of invulnerability had developed as a result of regulative aspects of the institutional environment, backed by powerful sanctions, norms, and rules. The workers' behavior was a function of how they interpreted the environment, and these processes had established a collective taken-for-granted understanding and attitude that created a reinforcing set of institutional expectations. A harmful mindset had become institutionalized: individual perceptions of the inherent risks in work practices had become clouded. The result was catastrophic.

A SYMBOLIC FORM DOMINATED BY BUREAUCRATIC LOGICS

Logics and level of refraction are two important concepts in Cassirer's theory. If the modern institution has gained such a strong position that it deserves to be called a symbolic form, it should also have developed explanations as well as focus areas that can be said to be typical of institutions. However, symbolic forms are dynamic and always in the making, and they are also influenced by and have integrated elements from other symbolic forms. In our daily lives, the boundaries between the symbolic forms are not absolute. On the contrary; the forms permeate each other, and they may have related logics. We may find traces of the logics of art in science, we find myth in art, and language and science build on similar processes of abstraction. Symbolic forms do not exist independently from each other, except in their ideal, pure forms.

So, if we are to understand the institution as a symbolic form, we should not expect to identify this form as something totally different from other forms. On the contrary, we should find characteristics that are distinct for, but not necessarily exclusive to, institutions. Within institutions, the logics of myths, history, language, art, science, and even religion contribute to the complex and dynamic blend that makes organizations into institutions that (to the despair of many managers) are difficult to control.

Nonetheless, if the institution can be said to be a symbolic form, we should be able to identify some general features of institutional logics and preferred levels of refraction—ways of influencing their members that are typical of, if not totally restricted to, institutions. They should have certain logics (e.g., theories of action, ways of explaining, and modes of planning), as well as certain ways of directing members to attend to specific areas and to ignore others. Because Cassirer's reality is cloaked as well as revealed in symbolic forms (*PSF* 3: 1), it follows that seeing the institution as a symbolic form should help us see some aspects of reality more clearly, whereas other areas fall outside their illuminating light. It should simultaneously open and hide reality. Because the unilateral use of one symbolic form may take certain dimensions of reality out of sight, it follows that an unreflected belief in and application of institutional logics will contribute to the "habitual blindness" that restricts our capacity as practitioners of management, as Cassirer warned.

What is specific to the institution as a symbolic form? Is a general tendency or metastandard apparent when it comes to institutions, a standard for organizing that has achieved dominance and tends to be taken for granted? Such a tendency certainly does exist if we are to believe a group of scholars. In the Renaissance, productivity, not efficiency and standardized routines, was the ideal, Sennett (2008) claimed: Work took the time that was required in order to produce quality. The craftsman was motivated by the desire to do a job well for its own sake, not by the need to live up to system requirements. This has changed: Organizations have become bundles of standardized sets of responses to problems, March and Simon (1958) claimed more than fifty years ago, and the way we think about work, quality, and productivity have altered. Perrow (1970) concluded his research by stating that the tendency of modern organizations to lean towards routinizing, standardizing, and bureaucracy, is " . . . inherent in the nature of an industrial civilization" (179). Tsoukas and Chia (2002) depicted modern organizations along the same lines, saying that traditional organizational perspectives have been dominated by presumptions of stability, routine, and order. Their claims are in line with Shenhav and Weitz's (2000) study of how management ideas were "translated" at the end of the 1800s and the beginning of the 1900s from the technical sphere to the management of organizations by the new and successful profession of engineers, who were specialists in avoiding uncertainty.

In the last decades, we have seen an increasing celebration of flexibility, adaptability, and change, as well as flat and dynamic organizations (Thomas 1996). The rhetoric should not lead us to think that institutional pressure towards uncertainty avoidance has faded. When Røvik (1996, 1998) studied the diffusion of organizational recipes, he found that the bureaucratic organizational form was still dominating. It seems to survive and mold the many waves of management ideas and recipes that sweep organizations in a globalized economy. Røvik's findings look to be in line with several other writers, who claim that mechanistic and bureaucratic thinking and presumptions of control, stability, and prediction dominate in contemporary organizations (Hatch 1999; Orlikowski 1996; Tsoukas and Chia 2002; Wheatley 1992). Rhetoric may change, new ideas may spread, but institutional logics based on a long tradition of bureaucratic ideas seem to prevail and influence us in their silent ways.

A symbolic form directs our attention towards certain aspects of reality, and tends to hide others. Consequently, if it is a valid conclusion that bureaucracy has become a metastandard for organizing, it is thus important to consider what members tend to see and what they tend to ignore when their impressions are molded by institutional logics and levels of refraction. From a Japanese perspective, Nonaka (1991) claimed that the Western world tended to focus on what can be counted and coded; on "hard" knowledge that can be described systematically and stored in a computer; on routines and procedures that can be formulated; on linear, sequential plans with measurable goals; on formal organization structures and, as much as possible, generalizable principles. These are elements of the surface structure of organizations that we have discussed in previous chapters— phenomena that have achieved a dominant position as a result of a unilateral use of the eye of science. Of course, this is no surprise. According to

Cassirer, science has the undisputed position as the utmost expression of man's consciousness and cultural life. That we find surface phenomena in the core of the bureaucratic metastandard is just one more example of how natural science has influenced institutional logics more than any other symbolic form. This is supported by Nonaka (1991) as well as Wheatly (1992), who both explained our inclination toward bureaucratic and mechanistic organizational forms with a strong influence from the natural sciences in the Western world.

HOW INSTITUTIONS MOLD OUR EXPERIENCES

Nonaka (1991) described a disposition to look at organizations as if they were machines, where well-oiled machinery with standardized and predictable production is the underlying ideal picture. The basic presumptions are control, programming, objectivity, stability, and prediction (Hatch 1999; Orlikowski 1996; Tsoukas and Chia 2002). In a world celebrating change these values may seem outdated. But building organizations on ideas of bureaucracy, routinization, and standardization is inherent in modern organizations, and should instead be regarded as intelligent ways of influencing members so that uncertainties and variabilities of the environment can be reduced, according to Perrow (1970).

If the bureaucratic standard for organizing is an intelligent way of influencing members, it does not necessarily imply that bureaucracy is an effective lens when it comes to understanding how these processes of influence take place and their potential dysfunctions.

As Levinthal (1991) pointed out, processes of institutionalization and creation of standardized routines form the basis of organizational continuity. One consequence of the bureaucratic metastandard's way of exercising power upon the actor in order to secure continuity is that deviation from the established standards and routines in general is not welcomed. Ignoring feelings and emotions in organizations will therefore be treacherous. An experience may have created a soma that in a similar situation triggers an automatic emotional response that tells us to disregard the deviation. The result may be habitual blindness, which can be utterly dangerous. As Wicks (2001) concluded after his study of the 1992 explosion at Westray Mines, in an industry like underground mining, the blindness created by reinforcing sets of institutional expectations can have catastrophic consequences; in many organizations, however, their negative consequences can easily go unnoticed year after year, but still be harmful. So even though change and learning well may be celebrated officially, the tendency of institutional forces to draw towards stability often is so strong and so subtle that it overrides the espoused values. Like Karl Weick (1991), one may speculate, "Perhaps organizations are not built to learn. Instead, they are patterns of means-ends relations deliberately designed to make the same routine response to different stimuli, a pattern which is antithetical to learning in the traditional sense" (119).

To understand and recognize the effects of institutional forces more fully, we could gain from drawing on the theory of symbolic forms backed by neurobiologists' research. Members in formal organizations learn through experience that deviation from the dominating bureaucratic metastandard in general is not welcomed (Irgens and Hernes 2008). It is the effect of symbolic pregnance that we see in play, the consequence of how the organization exercises power upon the actor when it becomes an institution. The actor experiences the institutional forces through immediate sensations in concrete situations. These experiences result in emotional traces or soma, in bodily memory associated with the situation. When we encounter related situations later, the established soma causes us to react unreflectively, and to shun or get closer to the situation at hand. As a culture philosopher, Cassirer called attention to the importance of aesthetic understanding and challenged us to develop the eye of art in order to understand these immediate sensory experiences. As a neurobiologist, Damasio pointed to the importance of emotions and warned us against ignoring their subtle effects. Both claimed that a unilateral use of science may result in a dangerous disregard of important aspects of human behavior that may confine our efforts to develop morally sound communities.

CHALLENGING THE HEGEMONY

Cassirer's philosophy encourages us to apply multiple symbolic forms, and depicts science and art as two forms that have complementary qualities. As I have argued, the eye of science has a long-lasting dominance in management theory and practice. Trying to complement science with the humanities and art will therefore challenge the dominating logics. Understanding the institution as a symbolic form may then help us understand the challenges of applying alternative logics in organizations. Jazz, the music form that is most often connected with the concept of improvisation, represents logics very different from the uncertainty avoidance logics that characterize modern institutions. One might say that the ideal picture in the bureaucratic metastandard lies much closer to Souza marches and military tattoos than to jazz. In a military tattoo, an enormous band with brass players and drums performs military marches that are strictly coordinated and structured. The intention is to maintain collective control. Any need that arises for improvising is regarded as a sign of weakness. Everything must be well-prepared and carried out with such strict choreography that the need for improvisation will never arise.

We have already seen that studies of expertise identify improvisation as a hallmark of the expert practitioner. Also, many organizational theorists have argued that formal planning and forecasting in our uncertain times must be replaced by improvisation and exploration (Brown and Eisenhardt 1997; Hatch 1999; Kamoche and Cunha 2001; Montuori 2003; Moorman and Miner 1998). In Chapter 6, I referred to the "Janus face" of organizational improvisation: we cannot avoid it, but at the same time that it solves local problems, it may create serious difficulties for other members and departments; and it challenges the official programs and plans because it represents a deviation from the status quo and standardized mode of production. Routines and standards are supraindividual and inhibit the logics of modern institutions (Weick 1991; Weick and Gilfillan 1971). Symbolic forms, and the modern institution regarded as a symbolic form, are objective in the sense that they exist on a supraindividual level: they mold our experiences and influence our behavior, but they also offer us the possibility of opening up, illuminating, and understanding the conditions that restrict our lives.

The dominating uncertainty-reducing logics of institutions do not favor improvisation or other creative and artistic ways of working. But at the same time that these logics aim at solving or helping us avoid organizational problems, they also produce problems that force actors to improvise (Dressman 1997). Thus, some scholars have argued for the need to apply playful and creative techniques when existing prescriptions do not work (Clegg, McManus, Smith, and Todd 2006; Starr-Glass and Schwartzbaum 2003). March (1976), for example, argued that we should go beyond rationality and purpose, because "foolish" behavior may open the possibility for new solutions. This is what ethnographers call *liminal behavior*. Liminality is often regarded as "being on a threshold," in a state or process betwixt and between the normal and the unknown or unusual (Turner 1979: 465). However, liminal behavior and liminal situations are dependent on context. Whereas foolish behavior, play, and other forms of liminal behavior may be both expected and welcomed in an informal familiy gathering (e.g., at a party, in a carnival, or in rites of passage), and improvisation is expected in a jazz band, the same behavior would challenge the existing order and provoke the established hegemony in most formal organizational settings.

The intrainstitutional effect of bureaucratic organizations at the same time produces liminal spaces *and* makes people feel guilty if they recognize liminality and react with liminal behavior (Cunha and Cabral-Cardoso 2006). The expectation of continuity and permanence force organizational members into liminality, but they also drive the same members to ignore or avoid liminal situations because of these situations' low degree of legitimacy. Coping with these dilemmas through foolishness, play, improvisation, or rule-breaking therefore tends to be sanctioned, confined, or subjected to self-censorship (Irgens and Hernes 2008). Bateson, Jackson, Haley, and Weakland (1956) would probably have called them double-blind situations produced by institutional forces. When the institutional expectation is strong towards permanence and uncertainty avoidance, managers tend to feel guilty when they find themselves engaged in deviance (Veiga, Golden, and Dechant 2004), and they may find themselves caught in a vicious circle of caution, blame, lack of reflection, and unproductive communication (Vince and Saleem 2004). Guilt is, in fact, normal, because even morally correct deviation still is a deviation in a bureaucratic organization (Cunha and Cabral-Cardoso 2006).

The modern institution as a symbolic form molds our experiences and influences our behavior in often subtle ways. Relying too much on the eye of science may gradually lead to a blindness that hinders us from seeing the effect of these forces. One of the strengths of the humanities is that they may help us unveil and better understand such forces and the dilemmas they oft create. Jazz can help us understand the relationship between rule following and improvisation, ethnography how liminal situations create dilemmas, culture theory how local ideologies establish hegemony and excersise power, and philosophy how we may develop critical thinking, just to mention a few examples. Leaving out these channels to reality confine our knowledge to organizational surface phenomena. We become semantic readers of organizations and victims of strategies, as the famous novelist and semiotician Umberto Eco put it:

> The former (semantic reader) uses the work as semantic machinery and is the victim of the strategies of the author who will lead him little by little along the series of previsions and expectations. The latter (semiotic reader) evaluates the work as an aesthetic product and enjoys the strategies implemented in order to produce a Model Reader of the first level (that is, a semantic reader). (Eco 1990: 92, in Czarniawska 1997: 69)

The rise of the modern institution may have been based on an assumption of a Model Worker whose main task is to carry out given strategies. Such a Model Worker has no need to understand organizations in other ways than merely superficial: Semantic reading is sufficient. However; in a society where knowledge intensive work seems to be increasingly valued, superficial knowledge is not sufficient. The new Model Worker needs a rich and realistic picture and the skills of the semiotic reader who is capabel of reading the organization as a multilevelled construct.

What we may achieve from understanding the institution as a symbolic form is a question that deserves thorough inquiry. From this piece of writing, I only make a few suggestions. First, I think, it may help us see the strengths and the weaknesses of institutions' specific levels of refraction and particular logics, both when applied as a channel to understand organizational phenomena and processes, and when applied outside the world of formal organizations where other symbolic forms dominate. Second, I think it may help us see how different symbolic forms coexist and influence behavior in organizations, as well as how we may gain a better and more realistic picture of organizations if we become proficient in understanding organizations through and as different forms. Third, it may help us develop curricula that are more realistic and fuller of life, where uncertainty, emotions, and feelings are both acknowledged and queried. In order to succeed, we need both the eye of science and the eye of art.

ON EDUCATION, PLURALISM, AND UNITY

"Human knowledge is by its very nature symbolic knowledge," Cassirer wrote (*EoM*: 57). This uniqueness makes humans capable of differentiating between what is real and what is possible, between the actual and the ideal world. Animals are confined within their world of sense perceptions, whereas humans live in a symbolic world where there is an epistemological difference between actuality and possibility. Mastering symbols is our key to the truly human world. Symbols are continually produced as a result of the development of the consciousness of man. Being part of a culture thus means being under the continual influence of historically developed symbolic forms that are mediating our daily experiences through symbolic pregnance. Without these forms, we will not have access to reality unless in the way of a tribesman: an expert as long as he is navigating in concrete space, but totally lost when asked to handle abstract spatial relations (*EoM*: 46). Symbolic forms both create and give us admission to the symbolic universe that characterizes human culture. Being restricted to one of these forms, or more correctly, relying too much on only one, will give us access only to a segment of the human world. We then develop blindness. A richer and more realistic picture will only emerge through prolific use of a breadth of forms.

Helping students develop a rich and realistic access to the world should accordingly be the main goal for our education systems. It should also be the most important goal for management education. Complex organizations are indeed appropriate examples of abstract, symbolic space, and should not be led by managers with oversimplified worldviews. In this book I have argued with Cassirer that art and science as symbolic forms have complementary qualities and that there is a need for developing curricula that builds and draws on the best of both forms. To avoid management education becoming merely technique, whether techniques for analyzing, calculating and using spreadsheets, or techniques for creativity, imagination and improvisation, there is a need for unveiling the underlying assumptions of the two traditions, which we find in the natural sciences and the humanities, respectively. That is; students need to learn how these traditions differ as ways of knowing; where they tend to focus, which values they build on, what characterizes their logics, how they can be applied differently, and so on. Only then can you hope for developing in the students some of the humility that great leaders sometimes display.[5] If, on the contrary, students leave school taking one and only one way of knowing for granted, we educate managers that will have serious problems in understanding other views, who will struggle imagining alternatives, and who will run into more and more problems the more complex an organization turns. And that counts whether their dominant way of knowing is the eye of art or the eye of science.

However, it is the eye of science that has gained dominance in management education. In its pure, ideal form, science does not allow room for other forms as ways of knowing. The irony is that to fully understand science, the logic of science, the role of science, and how it upholds its dominant position within organizational theory and management education, you will get a richer answer if drawing on other forms such as myth, history, language, and art. One of the great myths in management is in fact the assumption that organizations can be controlled through the eye of science. As I have tried to illustrate in this book, this myth may lead to blindness, to oversimplification, to unethical conduct, and to incapability when it comes to coping with complexity.

An alternative to hegemonic dominance is pluralism. Cassirer claimed that employing plural forms makes us better at navigating in complex space. But how can pluralism help us cope with complexity and turn us into better practitioners? Will we, contrary to what Cassirer claimed, end up with even more complexity, chaotic impressions, multitude of interpretations, chaos, and loss of direction?

We certainly will if the plural forms lack unification. However, according to Cassirer, the symbolic forms constitute a common, unifying context, and a unity of consciousness, even if the process that leads to understanding takes the form of "unconscious inference" (*PSF* 1: 104). The myriad of fluid impressions we have to make sense of in our daily lives assume form and duration for us when we mold them by symbolic action through formative processes, and a " . . . true unity of consciousness, as a unity of time, space, objective synthesis, etc." emerges (*PSF* 1: 102).

This is on the one hand pluralism: a diversity of forms, but they are held together by a unity of meaning. Through symbolic pregnance this unification process takes place immediately. That pluralism may be held together by unification is illustrated in the studies of experts. When we progress towards the level of expertise that Schön (1987, 1991), Berliner (2004), Dreyfus and Dreyfus (2005), and others claim characterize the best among us, we develop intuitive but at the same time realistic, rich, and functional representations of the situations we are facing. A unification takes place spontaneously, but not on the expense of richness. The result is representations that are not fragmented, but rather concentrated images that reduce our cognitive load. This in turn makes us better at prediction. As I claimed in Chapter 6, this capacity to interpret complex situations and "read" the organization, and to predict what then might happen, is probably the most sought-after capacity in today's complex and dynamic organizations. That should count for managers as well.

In other words, managers need to learn to "see" the organization, and interpretation becomes the key word if we want to develop excellent managers. Developing rich and realistic understanding of the world is the challenge of all and not only management education, if we follow Cassirer.

BRINGING IN THE HUMANITIES

"After years of seeking these Holy Grails, it is time to recognize that managing is neither a science nor a profession; it is a practice, learned primarily through experience, and rooted in context."

These are the words of Henry Mintzberg (2009: 9). Managing is certainly not a science, he concluded after having observed a number of managers in their daily practice. Managers do not develop systematic knowledge through science: "Managing is not even an applied science, because that is still science" (10). Managers do certainly apply knowledge they may get from science, following Mintzberg; and they analyze in a tradition rooted in the scientific method. However; effective managing relies more on art, Mintzberg held forth: Art draws on intuition and may result in insights and vision. But to Mintzberg, managing is first of all a practice: "Put together a good deal of craft with the right touch of art alongside some use of science, and you end up with a job that is above all a *practice*" (10).

Managing becomes a mix of science, art, and craft, according to Mintzberg, who has also developed a scale by which managers can assess their personal style of management. A preference for ideas, intuition, heart, strategies, inspiring, passionate, novel, seeing it, "the possibilities are endless" means that you belong in the art camp. Experiences, practical, hands, processes, engaging, helpful, realistic, learning, doing it, "consider it done" are related to craft. A preference for facts, analytical, head, outcomes, informing, reliable, determined, organizing, thinking it, "that's perfect" mean that you rely primarily on science.

So far so good. Management is according to Mintzberg science as well, after all, and it is art and craft, and together they constitute the practice of managing. This is how Minztberg concludes after observing managers closely. The problem is that Mintzberg delimits management to a contextual practice that is primarily learned through experience. In earlier writings he has also expressed his skepticism towards teaching young students management: "Using the classroom to help develop people already practicing management is a fine idea, but pretending to create managers out of people who have never managed is a sham" (Mintzberg 2004: 5). This is where Mintzberg and Cassirer seem to part: Because symbolic forms constitute practice, the same practice can be improved through enhancing our capability to apply and combine forms, if we are to follow Cassirer. Good practice can be learned, not only in the context of work organizations, but also through education.[6] That should also apply to the practice of managing.

But a closer reading of Mintzberg reveals that the difference might not be as big as it first seems. Mintzberg criticizes the business schools' tendency to reduce management education to technique: managing is reduced to decision making, decision-making is reduced to analysis, and analysis is reduced to technique (Mintzberg 2004: 38–39). We end up educating the mathematical manager that lacks soft skills. Cassirer would probably agree, and say that this is the result of the dominance of the eye of science in MBA programs.

Mintzberg points to the problematic task of teaching inexperienced students soft skills. It can't be done through teaching, and the solution is neither the case study method. Teaching soft skills requires deep reflection that in turn requires real world experience from a managerial context.

Whereas Cassirer calls for the eye of art to complement the eye of science, Mintzberg calls for the soft skills. Among Wikipedia's examples of soft skills, are *socializing with someone, unite a team amidst cultural differences, teach others, coach others, motivate others, negotiate, active listening, foresee situations, empathic communication, self-awareness,* as well as *proactive attitude.* Now we are talking about the humanities, rather than the natural sciences. So if you are to *study* soft skills, and not only *practice* soft skills, you have to go to the humanities. Soft skills are about interpretation, imagination, sensitivity, ethics, creativity, and meaning. Soft skills are a way of putting the eye of art into practice.

We do not live in a world of hard facts alone or according to immediate needs and desires, as Cassirer maintained; but in a world of imaginary emotions, hopes and fears, illusions and disillusions, and among our fantasies and our dreams (*EoM*: 25). This is a world where we cannot succeed without soft skills. If we are to create a basis for good management through education, we thus need to draw on the knowledge of interpretation and imagination that is developed through the humanities, *as well as* the tradition building on the values and preferences of the natural sciences. Liberal education has to be included in, and related to, the teaching of the hard skills that, according to Mintzberg and many others, dominates management education.

LET'S JUST GIVE UP (OR MAYBE NOT?)

Cassirer was able to conceive of philosophy as the interpretation of culture only because he shared with most of his generation a conception of culture itself as an essentially liberating force. The twentieth century was not kind to that idea. The cancerous growth of bureaucracy, the murderous perversion of science, the self-prostitution of the humanities—none of this portended liberation. The younger generation accordingly sought a standard of truth over and above culture's shifting tides. The logical positivists found it in the verification principle,

Heidegger in authentic existence. Others turned to the Bible or the wisdom of ancient Greece. All agreed that the humanism of the past two centuries had failed (Skidelsky 2008: 6)

The humanities have faced many crises (Kagan 2010; Nussbaum 2009; Slingerland 2010). Some of them may have been, at least partially, self-induced. But today, after Enron, the collapse of financial institutions, the corrosion of character, the many global crises, and the growing mistrust in leaders and institutions we need the best of the humanities more than ever.

However; bringing in the best of the humanities is challenging. First; the humanities are about values and ideals that seem to be anachronistic in today's business world where short-term profit motives and a structural view of organizations seem to hold a strong stance. Accordingly; it will take time and will require willingness of all parts to make the required changes. Second, just "bringing the humanities in" would be an important step, but it is not sufficient to establish interpretive skills in management education. Just bringing the humanities in as a supplement would probably raise the students' level of Socratic self-criticism and critical thought, it would improve their capacity to see themselves as members of a heterogeneous world, and it would also strengthen their "narrative imagination," all values that according to Nussbaum are particularly crucial to decent global citizenship (Nussbaum 2009: 10). However, if we are to develop the two-eyed capacity that Cassirer called for, we need to see where and how the eye of art and the eye of science may complement each other in such a way that a new insight in and understanding of management and organizations emerges. We also need to find ways to teach management so that the complementarities of the two eyes become evident. Good work has been done, but it is way too little, and the efforts have been far too fragmented. In order to avoid fragmented efforts, there is a need for bringing the two main camps in management theory and practice together in fruitful dialogue. A new dialogue would probably benefit both parties, and certainly the students of management, as I have argued throughout this book. As Edward G. Slingerland puts it,

Bringing the humanities and the natural sciences together into a single, integrated chain seems to me the only way to clear up the current miasma of endlessly contingent discourses and representations of representations that currently hampers humanistic inquiry. By the same token, as natural scientists begin poking their noses into areas traditionally studied by the humanities—the nature of ethics, literature, consciousness, emotions, or aesthetics—they are sorely in need of humanistic expertise if they are to effectively decide what sorts of questions to ask, how to frame these questions, and what sorts of stories to tell in interpreting their data. (Slingerland 2010: Loc. 408–417)

"Bringing the humanities and the natural sciences together" may seem like an insurmountable challenge in the modern Academy where, according to Slingerland, the split between these two ways of knowing has been institutionalized and the faculty is located in separate departments. Bringing biologists and physicists together with jazz musicians and ethnographers is not necessarily productive in any sense if there is no common cause to concentrate on. But the divide that Friedman (2000) pointed to in philosophy is also found within the walls of many management departments and in the very same conferences. Here we have a common cause, namely, the quality of research and teaching. Just coming together in order to start discussing our often taken for granted assumptions and their consequences for method at large, including how we educate managers, would be a good beginning.

In that case we would benefit from a non-dualistic and relational theory. I think Friedman (2000: 159) was right when he said that Ernst Cassirer is a good place to start. But we also need to develop two-eyed textbooks, two-eyed curricula, and two-eyed designs for classroom learning. It may sound like share naivety, and it might be tempting just to give up. On the other side, there once was a fruitful dialogue between very different camps. So maybe we should give it a try, after all.

Notes

NOTES TO CHAPTER 2

1. Dualism may have many meanings. Here, by non-dualistic I refer to a theory that does not detach body from mind, or reality from mind. Cassirer stressed relationship, not separation. For a discussion of dualism, see Searle (2002).
2. The distinction between nomotetic and idiographic knowledge stems from the Baden school's Wilhelm Windelband, according to Birkeland (1993: 7).
3. For more on symbolic pregnance, see Chapter 7.
4. Although Cassirer found Vico's theory of the development of language both strange and baroque, he also asserted that Vico's theory offered a fruitful approach to inquiry into the problem of language. Feelings and emotions lay the foundation for speech, which in turn was the basis for language. When the eighteenth century, after nearly two decades of celebrating rationality, turned from rationality to feelings, Vico's theory of the origin of language became important again, and was picked up by Rousseau, among others.
5. In a review of Skidelsky (2008), Peter E. Gordon writes that Cassirer never had been a philosopher to arouse much enthusiasm, and that even in his own time a respectful colleague such as Karl Jaspers could tell his peers that "Cassirer bores me." Some of Cassirer's most successful students," Gordon continues, "such as the political philosopher Leo Strauss or the theorist of metaphor and modernity Hans Blumenberg, utterly revised much of what Cassirer hoped to achieve." Rudolf Carnap characterized Cassirer as "rather pastoral," Isaiah Berlin judged him "serenely innocent," and Adorno— "never one to mince words," Gordon reminds us—called him "totally gaga." Gordon quotes Skidelsky (2008: 7): "Cassirer's 'thought remains, when all is said and done, a stranger to our age'" (*Notre Dame Philosophical Reviews*, http://ndpr.nd.edu/review.cfm?id=17346. Accessed July 6 2010.).

NOTES TO CHAPTER 3

1. In the second volume of *The Philosophy of Symbolic Forms*, Cassirer mentioned ethics, law, economics, and technology as possible symbolic forms.
2. Lewin argued that social phenomena are real, and built on Cassirer when he asserted that there is
   > ... no more magic behind the fact that groups have properties of their own, which are different from the properties of their subgroups and their individual members, than behind the fact that molecules have properties, which are different from the properties of the atoms or ions of which they are composed. (Lewin 1947: 8)

He continued to build on Cassirer when he maintained that structural properties " . . . are characterized by *relations* between parts rather than by the parts or elements themselves," and made a case for a combination of "subjective" and "objective methods" (30–31).

3. John R. Searle is in line with Cassirer when he writes, " . . . institutional structures have a special feature, namely, symbolism. The biological capacity to make something symbolize—or mean, or express—something beyond itself is the basic capacity that underlies not only language but all other forms of institutional reality as well" (Searle 1995: 228). See Chapter 7 for more for more on the modern institution as a symbolic form.

4. I am thankful to one of my anonymous reviewers who pointed out that Cassirer wrongly named von Uexküll *Johannes*, a mistake that has survived many later editions. *Jakob* is the correct first name.

5. It seems like it is the opposite that is taking place in education: "The humanities and arts are being cut away, in both primary/secondary and college/university education, in virtually every nation in the world," according to Martha Nussbaum (2010: 2).

6. *Substanzbegriff und Funktionsbegriff. Untersuchungen über die Grundfragen der Erkenntniskritik* (1910).

7. Abbreviated "*LoH*."

8. First published in 1942 as "*Zur Logik der Kulturwissenschaften. Fünf Studien.*"

9. Slingerland (2010: Loc. 295–303) claims that this split between two different types of knowing about the world has been institutionalized in the modern Academy.

10. This, and concepts such as *Geist* and *Wissenschaft*, surely have put translators on serious tests: In the translator's foreword to Cassirer's *The Logic of the Humanities*, Clarence Smith Howe devotes most of his 12-page forward on trying to decode the German tradition to the English-speaking audience. He warns that "(. . .) the Kulturwissenschaften, for which Cassirer and his predecessors are seeking the basic logic, are not to be facilely identified with what the English-speaking world refers to as 'the social sciences.'" Howe holds forth that the German concept of science (*Wissenschaft*) is much broader than its English counterpart: "In this wider meaning, 'science' is not concerned with factual descriptions and the exact lawful relationships obtaining between natural events. Rather, it is science in the ancient sense of being a profounder or more adequate knowledge of what we already 'know' in the factual sense of our direct and daily encounter of the world and ourselves. Thus, even poetry and mythology can be the concern of that disciplined knowledge which is Kulturwissenschaft. It is precisely for this reason that I have chosen to translate Kulturwissenschaften as 'the humanities'" (Howe 1961: xiii–xiv).

11. Instead of writing about *leaders* and *leadership*, I primarily apply the terms *managers* and *management*. I do agree with Mintzberg (2009) that leadership has been pushed off the map and that an artificial delineation has been drawn between managers and leaders.

12. Paetzold (2002–1) stated,

> If we take Cassirer's assumption seriously that modernity started in the Renaissance period and not in Cartesian rationalism, then we may even find access to contemporaneous debates about modernity and postmodernity. I believe that the latter is a serious subject for the philosophy of culture, since epochal breaks and cuts in which our cultural self-understanding is challenged are at stake here. If Cassirer is right when arguing that modernity started in the Renaissance period, then, I

think, modernity and postmodernity are not related to each other such as two different planets, but rather by way of accelerated transformation. (54)

13. The participants in the 1928 series included Jean Piaget and Paul Tillich. In 1929, Emmanuel Levinas, Rudolph Carnap, Erich Maria Remarque, and Otto Freidrich von Bollnow were among the participants.

14. "*Die unterschiedlichen Auffassungen von Kants 'Kritik der reinen Vernunft,' die sich am deutlichsten in der Entgegensetzung von menschlichen Endlichkeit (Heidegger) und der prinzipiellen Unendlichkeit menschlichen Geistes und menschlicher Produktivität (Cassirer) ausdrücken, stehen im Mittelpunkt des Disputes*" (Meyer 2006: 172).

NOTES TO CHAPTER 4

1. According to Elster, the social sciences, " . . . which I define so broadly as to include linguistics, history, and psychology in addition to the more obvious disciplines" (Elster 1983:15), and the aesthetic disciplines or art are subcategories of the humanities.

2. A second challenge is the use of concepts. As Jerome Kagan (2010) discusses, the meanings of the vocabularies are very different in the humanities and the natural sciences.

3. Admittedly, the manner in which Putnam used the category functionalism is far from exact. Boal, Hunt, and Jaros (2004), for example, argue that positivists are not necessarily "functionalists." They claim that positivists were strongly critical of drawing parallels between functional explanations and functionalism, as well as between biological and social systems, and assert that if contemporary science or management theory is functionalist, it is not positivist.

4. This use of the term "functionalistic" may be confusing, as it is used in a broader and less precise sense than usual (e.g., as it is described by Andersen 1990: 49).

5. Other contributions in organization theory were made by Morgan (1988, 1991), Arbnor and Bjerke (1977), Bolman and Deal (1991), Gioia and Pitre (1990), Knights and Mueller (2004), as well as Boisot and McKelvey's "Integrating Modernist and Postmodernist Perspectives on Organizations" (forthcoming).

6. With some prominent exceptions such as Nelson Goodman, Krois held forth. Dag Østerberg (2002) analyzed constructivist sociology from the viewpoint of Cassirer's philosophy, from the school closest to common sense, via what he called the path-breaking work of Bourdieu and Foucault, to the extreme forms of social constructivism, and concluded, "As the examinations approached the more extreme constructivist positions, Cassirer's thought appeared less congenial—a finding that may cast some doubt on Cassirer's thought, but even more doubt upon these extreme varieties of social constructivism" (92).

NOTES TO CHAPTER 5

1. As we have seen, Verene (1969: 36) claimed that Cassirer built his idea of symbolic forms on Hegel, rather than on Kant. However, this does not imply that Cassirer did not draw on Kant as well.

2. For alternative interpretations, see (Dunn, Dalgleish, and Lawrence 2006; Maia and McClelland 2004; Maia and McClelland, 2005).

3. There have been presented other ways of interpreting the Iowa card game experiment (Maia and McClelland 2004).
4. Damasio (2001) suggested that the terms "emotion" and "feelings" should not be used interchangeably (103). "Emotions" should be used to designate a collection of responses that are triggered from the brain or, more specifically, from parts of the brain to the body, as well as from parts of the brain to other parts of the brain. The result of the collection of responses is an *emotional state*. This state is defined in changes in the body proper and within particular sectors of the brain. "Feelings" is a term that should be used to describe complex mental states that result from the emotional states.
5. Among the exceptions, Damasio mentions Charles Darwin, William James, and Sigmund Freud.
6. This seems parallel to Cassirer's (1944) claim that science leads to abstraction and thus to an impoverishment of reality through reduction, classification, and analysis (149).
7. NRK—The Norwegian Broadcasting Corporation 4 December 2003.
So is Searle: "On my view the traditional opposition that we tend to make between biology and culture is as misguided as the traditional opposition between mind and body (Searle 1995: 227).

NOTES TO CHAPTER 6

1. When Edward Skidelsky, the Cassirer scholar, reviewed Blink by Malcolm Gladwell he criticized Gladwell's rather uncritical celebration of intuition and pointed out that there " . . . is no such thing, in short, as a free-floating faculty of intuition." http://www.telegraph.co.uk/culture/books/3636444/ Good-intuition-takes-years-of-practice.html Accessed October 25, 2010.
2. Berliner (2004) quoted the great hockey player Wayne Gretsky. When asked for the secret of his fantastic success, Gretsky answered: "I don't know; I just go to where the puck is going to be."
3. Accessed Oct 23, 2003. http://drawright.com/
4. It is also illustrative that none of the twelve contributions to Linstead and Höpfl's *The Aesthetics of Organization* (2000) refers to Cassirer or his works.
5. As Elster (1983) pointed out, the very notion of "social systems" is in itself debatable.
6. So does the study of macro-processes of organizations, according to Lex Donaldson (2005), a convinced representative of a positivistic organizational science.
7. ECTS is the European Credit Transfer System, a standard for degree credits and grades according to the Bologna Convention.
8. Member checks is a method for having actors from the empirical field correct hypotheses and validate findings (Bryman 1988; Swanborn 1996). One experienced faculty member that I had read through the chapter commented that the MKL case also could have been analyzed by applying personality theory, for example when it comes to understanding disagreements between faculty members. Whereas I agree that both personality theory and a series of other theories could have been chosen to inform the case, I have deliberately selected to stick to the main theme of this book and focus on the consequences of different forms of knowing.

NOTES TO CHAPTER 7

1. C. P. Snow's "two cultures," Gidden's structuration theory, Hodkinson's philosophy of leadership, Bourdieu's work, and recently Boisot and McKelvey are just a few examples.
2. The latter, incidentally, bears a resemblance to what some scholars have pointed out also applies to Karl Weick's writing (Van Maanen 1995).
3. Notice the similarities between Pierre Bourdieu's (1990) theory of *habitus* and Cassirer's symbolic form: *habitus* is a predisposition that mediates the relationship between the individual and society. Bourdieu acknowledges Cassirer as one of the inspirations for his own work.
4. There are many ways of regarding institutions. Some voices also claim that organizations should not be seen as institutions. I will not dwell on these problematics in this piece of writing, but I recommend Hodgson (2006) for a discussion.
5. See, for example, Marika Griehsel's interview with Desmond Tutu, the South African activist, bishop, and Nobel Peace price laureate; http://nobelprize. org/
6. Education can be understood as an introduction to the specificities of symbolic codings that belong to the particular culture, according to Paetzold (2002-1: 50–51), an introduction that leads to symbolic pregnance

Bibliography

Adler, N. (2006) The arts and leadership: Now that we can do anything, what will we do? *Academy of Management Learning & Education*, 5, 486–499.

Alterhaug, B. (2004) Improvisation on a triple theme: Creativity, jazz improvisation and communication. *Studia Musicologica Norvegica*, 30, 97–118.

Alvesson, M. and Willmott, H. (1992) *Critical Theory and Management Studies: An Introduction*. London: Sage.

Amabile, T. M. (1996) *Creativity in Context*. Boulder, CO: Westwood Press.

Andersen, H., ed. (1990) *Videnskabsteori og metodelære*. Vol. 2, Erhvervsøkonomi. Frederiksberg, Denmark: Samfundslitteratur.

Ansoff, H. I. (1991) Critique of Henry Mintzberg's "The design school: Reconsidering the basic premises of strategic management." *Strategic Management Journal*, 12, 449–461.

Arbnor, I. and Bjerke, B. (1977) *Företaksekonomisk metodlära*. Lund, Sweden: Studentlitteratur.

Argyris, C., Putnam, R. and McLain Smith, D. (1985) *Action Science. Concepts, Methods and Skills for Research and Intervention*. San Francisco: Jossey Bass.

Argyris, C. and Schön, D. (1978) *Organizational Learning: A Theory of Action Perspective*. Reading, MA: Addison-Wesley.

Augier, M. 2004. *March on leadership, education, and Don Quixote: Introduction and interview*. Academy of Management Learning and Education, 3(2), 169–177.

Austin, R. and Devin, L. (2003) *Artful Making: What Managers Need to Know About How Artists Work*. New York: Prentice Hall.

Barrett, F. J. and Peplowski, K. (1998) Minimal Structures Within a Song: An Analysis of "All of Me." *Organization Science*, 9(5), 558–560.

Barry, D. (1996) Artful inquiry: A symbolic constructivist approach to social science research. *Qualitative Inquiry*, 2, 411–438.

Barry, D. (2008) "The art of . . . ," in D. Barry and H. Hansen (Eds.) *The Sage Handbook of New Approaches in Management and Organization*. London: Sage, 31–41.

Barry, D. and Hansen, H. (2008) *The Sage Handbook of New Approaches in Management and Organization*. London: Sage.

Basbøll, T. and Graham, H. (2006) Substitutes for strategy research: Notes on the source of Karl Weick's anecdote of the young lieutenant and the map of the Pyrenees. *Ephemera*, 6(2), 194–204.

Bateson, G., Jackson, D. D., Haley, J. and Weakland, J. (1956) Toward a theory of schizophrenia. *Behavioral Science*, 1, 251–264.

Bayer, T. I. (2002) "Socratic self-knowledge and the philosophy of symbolic forms," in G. A. Magee (Ed.) *Philosophy and Culture: Essays in Honor of Donald Phillip Verene*. Charlottesville, VA: Philosophy Documentation Center, 85–103.

Bechara, A. and Damasio, A. R. (2005) The somatic marker hypothesis: A neural theory of economic decision. *Games and Economic Behavior*, 52, 336–372.

Berliner, D. C. (1994) "Expertise: The wonder of exemplary performances," in J. N. Mangieri and C. C. Block (Eds.) *Creating Powerful Thinkers in Teachers and Students*. Fort Worth, TX: Holt, Rinehart & Winston, 161–186.

Berliner, D. C. (2004) Describing the behavior and documenting the accomplishments of expert teachers. *Bulletin of Science, Technology, & Society*, 24(3), 200–212.

Bidney, D. (1949) "On the philosophical anthropology of Ernst Cassirer and its relation to the history of anthropological thought," in P. A. Schilpp (Ed.) *The Philosophy of Ernst Cassirer*. New York: Tudor, 467–544.

Birkeland, Å. (1993) *Cassirer-Rickert-Weber*. Oslo, Norway: University of Oslo.

Birkeland, Å. and Nilsen H. (2002) "Thinking in forms. Ernst Cassirer's critique of the nomothetic-idiographic distinction," in G. Foss and E. Kasa (Eds.) *Forms of Knowledge and Sensibility. Ernst Cassirer and the Human Sciences*. Kristiansand, Norway: Høyskoleforlaget, 93–118.

Boal, K. B., Hunt, J. G. and Jaros, S. J. (2004) "Order is free: On the ontological status of organizations," in R. Westwood and S. Clegg (Eds.) *Debating Organization: Point-Counterpoint in Organization Studies*. Oxford: Blackwell, 84–97.

Boisot, M. and McKelvey, B. (forthcoming) Integrating modernist and postmodernist perspectives on organizations: A complexity science bridge. *Academy of Management Review*.

Bolman, L. G. and Deal, T. E. (1991) *Reframing Organizations: Artistry, Choice and Leadership*. San Francisco: Jossey-Bass.

Borum, F. and Westenholz, A. (1995) "An incorporation of multiple institutional models: Organizational field multiplicity and the role of actors," in W. R. Scott and S. Christensen (Eds.) *The Institutional Construction of Organization*. London: Sage, 113–131.

Bourdieu, P. (1990) *The Logic of Practice*. Cambridge, England: Polity Press.

Brown, J. S. and Duguid, P. (2000) *The Social Life of Information*. Boston: Harvard Business School Press.

Brown, S. L. and Eisenhardt, K. M. (1997) The art of continuous change: Linking complexity theory and time-paced evolution in relentlessly shifting organizations. *Administrative Science Quarterly*, 42, 1–34.

Bryman, A. (1988) *Quantity and Quality in Social Research*. London: Unwin Hyman.

Budd, M. (1998) "Aesthetics," in E. Craig (Ed.) *Routledge Encyclopedia of Philosophy*. London: Routledge. Online. Available HTTP: <http://www.rep.routledge.com/article/M046> (accessed 24 November 2007).

Burrell, G. and Morgan, G. (1979) *Sociological Paradigms and Organizational Analysis*. London: Heinemann.

Carr, A. (2002) Art and aesthetics at work: An overview. *Tamara: Journal of Critical Postmodern Organization Science*. Online. Available HTTP: <http://findarticles.com/p/articles/mi_qa4007/is_200201/ai_n9036684/print> (accessed July 2003).

Cassirer, E. (1910) Substanzbegriff und Funktionsbegriff. *Untersuchungen über die Grundfragen der Erkenntniskritik*. Berlin: Bruno Cassirer.

Cassirer, E. (1916) *Freiheit und Form: Studien zur Deutschen Geistesgeschichte*. Berlin: Bruno Cassirer.

Cassirer, E. (1944) *An Essay on Man*. New Haven, CT: Yale University Press.

Cassirer, E. (1946) *The Myth of the State*. New Haven, CT: Yale University Press.

Cassirer, E (1951) *The Philosophy of the Enlightenment*. Princeton, NJ: Princeton University Press.

Cassirer, E. (1953) Language. Vol. 1 of *The Philosophy of Symbolic Forms*. New Haven, CT: Yale University Press.

Cassirer, E. (1955) Mythical Thought. Vol. 2 of *The Philosophy of Symbolic Forms*. New Haven, CT: Yale University Press.

Cassirer, E. (1957) The Philosophy of Knowledge. Vol. 3 of *The Philosophy of Symbolic Forms*. New Haven, CT: Yale University Press.

Cassirer, E. (1961) *Logic of the Humanities*. New Haven, CT: Yale University Press.

Cassier, E. (1996) The Philosophy of Symbolic Forms Vol. 4, *The Metaphysics of Symbolic Forms*. New Haven: Yale University Press (Edited by J. M. Krois and D. P. Verene).

Clegg, S., McManus, M., Smith, K. and Todd, M. J. (2006) Self-development in support of innovative pedagogies: Peer support using email. *International Journal for Academic Development*, 11, 91–100.

Cooper, R. (1992) "Formal organization as representation: Remote control, displacement and abbreviation," in M. Reed and M. Hughes (Eds.) *Rethinking Organization: New Directions in Organization Theory and Analysis*. London: Sage, 254–272.

Csikszentmihalyi, M. (1990) *Flow: The Psychology of Optimal Experience*. New York: Harper and Row.

Cunha, M. P. and Cabral-Cardoso, C. (2006) Shades of Gray: A Liminal Interpretation of Organizational Legality-Illegality. *International Public Management Journal*, 9, 209–225.

Czarniawska, B. (1997) *A narrative approach to organization studies*. Thousand Oaks, CA: Sage.

Czarniawska, B. (2003) Forbidden knowledge. Organization theory in times of transition. *Management Learning*, 34, 353–365.

Dalgleish, T. (2004) The emotional brain. *Cortex*, 14, 199–208.

Damasio, A. R. (1989) Concepts in the brain. *Mind and Language*, 4, 24–28.

Damasio, A. R. (1994) *Descartes' Error: Emotion, rationality and the human brain*. New York: Avon Books.

Damasio, A. R. (1999) *The Feeling of What Happens*. Heineman: London.

Damasio, A. R. (2001) Emotion and the human brain. *Annals of the New York Academy of Sciences*, 935, 101–106.

Damasio, A. R. (2003) *Looking for Spinoza: Joy, Sorrow, and the Feeling Brain*. New York: Harcourt.

Damasio, A. R., Everitt, B. J. and Bishop, D. (1996) The Somatic Marker Hypothesis and the Possible Functions of the Prefrontal Cortex [and Discussion]. *Philosophical Transactions: Biological Sciences*, 351, 1413–1420.

Darsø, L. (2004) *Learnin-Tales Of Arts-in-business*. Copenhagen, Denmark: Learning Lab Denmark.

Deetz, S. A. and Kersten, A. (1983) "Critical models of interpretive research," in L. Putnam and M. E. Pacanowsky (Eds.) *Communication and Organizations*. Beverly Hills: Sage, 147–172.

Dewey, J. (2005) *Art as Experience*. London: Penguin Books.

Donaldson, L. (2005) For positive management theories while retaining science: Reply to Ghoshal. *Academy of Learning & Education*, 4, 109–113.

Dressman, M. (1997) Congruence, resistance, liminality: Reading and ideology in three school libraries. *Curriculum Inquiry*, 27, 267–315.

Dreyfus, H. and Dreyfus, S. (2005) Expertise in real world contexts. *Organization Studies* 26(5), 779–792.

Dreyfus, H. L., Dreyfus, S. E. and Athanasiou, T. (1986) *Mind Over Machine: The Power of Human Intuition and Expertise in the Era of the Computer*. New York: Free Press.

Dunn, B. D., Dalgleish, T. and Lawrence, A. D. (2006) The somatic marker hypothesis: A critical evaluation. *Neuroscience and Biobehavioral Reviews*, 30, 239–271.

du Plessis, E. (2005) Advertisers' new insight into the brain. *Admap*, May, 20–23.

Edwards, B. (1979) *Drawing on the Right Side of the Brain*. Los Angeles: J. P. Tarcher.

Elster, J. (1983) *Explaining Technological Change: A Case Study in the Philosophy of Science*. Cambridge, England: Cambridge University Press.

Emirbayer, M. (1997) Manifesto for a relational sociology. *American Journal of Sociology*, 103, 281–317.

Ferrari, M. (2003) Ernst Cassirer: Stationen einer philosophischen Biographie. *Vor der Marburger Schule zur Kulturphilosophie*. Hamburg, Germany: Felix Meiner Verlag.

Fiol, C. M. and O'Connor, E. J. (2008) "Nurturing the divide: Toward maximizing the value of management research from both sides of the Atlantic," in D. Barry and H. Hansen (Eds.) *The Sage Handbook of New Approaches in Management and Organization*. London: Sage, 251–254.

Fleetwood, S. (2005) Ontology in organization and management studies: A critical realist perspective. *Organization*, 12, 197–222.

Foss, G. and Kasa, E. (2002) "Preface," in G. Foss and E. Kasa (Eds.) *Forms of Knowledge and Sensibility: Ernst Cassirer and the Human Sciences*. Kristiansand, Norway: Høyskoleforlaget, 9–17.

Friedlander, F. (1989) "Patterns of individual and organizational learning," in Suresh Srivastva and Associates (Ed.) *The Executive Mind*. San Francisco: Jossey Bass, 192–220.

Friedman, M. (2000) *A Parting of the Ways: Carnap, Cassirer, and Heidegger*. Chicago, IL: Open Court.

Friedman, M. (2002) Carnap, Cassirer, and Heidegger: The Davos disputation and twentieth century philosophy. *European Journal of Philosophy*, 10, 263–274.

Friedman, M. (2005) Ernst Cassirer and contemporary philosophy of science. *Angelaki: Journal of the Theoretical Humanities*, 10, 119–128.

Gadamer, H.-G. (1981) Den filosofiske hermeneutikk reflekterer over betingelsene for at forståelse overhode kan lykkes. Interview with Hans-Georg Gadamer. Dyade, 4, 29–47.

Gadamer, H.-G. (1989) *Truth and Method*. 2nd rev. edition. New York: Crossroad.

Gawronsky, D. (1949) "Ernst Cassirer: His life and his work. A biography," in P. A. Schilpp (Ed.) *The Philosophy of Ernst Cassirer*. New York: Tudor, 1–37.

Gergen, K. J. (1992) "Organization theory in the postmodern era," in M. Reed and M. Hughes (Eds.) *Rethinking Organizations*. London: Sage, 207–226.

Ghoshal, S. (2005) Bad theories are destroying good management practices. *Academy of Learning & Education*, 4, 75–91.

Gioia, D. A. and Pitre, E. (1990) Multiparadigm perspectives on theory building. *Academy of Management Review*, 15(4), 584–602.

Gladwell, M. (2005) *Blink: The Power of Thinking Without Thinking*. New York: Little, Brown and Company.

Goodman, N. (1978) *Ways of Worldmaking*. Indianapolis, IN: Hackett Publishing Company.

Gudykunst, W. B. and Kim, Y. Y. (1992) *Communicating with Strangers: An Approach to Intercultural Communication*. New York: McGraw-Hill.

Guillet de Monthoux, P., Gustafsson, C. and Sjöstrand, S.-E. (2007) *Aesthetic Leadership: Managing Fields of Flow in Art and Business*. New York: Palgrave Macmillan.

Habermas, J. (1982) *Theory of Communicative Action.* Oxford, England: Polity Press.

Habermas, J. (2001) *The Liberating Power of Symbols.* Cambridge, MIT: Philosophical Essays.

Hamburg, C. H. (1949) "Cassirer's Conception of Philosophy" in P. A. Schilpp (Ed.) *The Philosophy of Ernst Cassirer.* New York: Tudor, 73–120.

Hamlin, B., Keep, J. and Ash, K. (2001) *Organizational Change and Development: A Reflective Guide for Managers, Trainers and Developers.* Edinburgh, England: Pearson Education.

Hancock, P. (2002) Aestheticizing the world of organization—Creating beautiful untrue things. *Tamara: Journal of Critical Postmodern Organization Science.* Online. Available HTTP: <http://findarticles.com/p/articles/mi_qa4007/is_200201/ai_n9036684/print> (accessed 23 March 2006).

Hassard, J. (1996) "Exploring the terrain of modernism and postmodernism in organization theory," in D. M. Boje, R. P. Gephart and T. J. Thatchenkery (Eds.) *Postmodern Management and Organization Theory.* Thousand Oaks, CA: Sage, 45–59.

Hatch, M. J. (1999) Exploring the empty spaces of organizing: How improvisational jazz helps redescribe organizational structure. *Organization Studies,* 20(1), 75–100.

Higgins, C. (2001) From reflective practice to practical wisdom: Three models of liberal teacher education. *Philosophy of Education Yearbook 2001,* 92–99.

Hodgson, G. M. (2006) What Are Institutions? *Journal of Economic Issues,* 40, 1–25.

Hoel, A. S. (2006) "Innledning," in E. Cassirer (Ed.) *Form og Teknikk. Utvalgte Tekster.* Oslo, Norway: Cappelen Akademisk Forlag, 7–46.

Holub, M. (1977) Brief Thoughts on Maps. *Times Literary Supplement,* Feb 4, 118.

Howe, C. S. (1961) "Translator's foreword," in E. Cassirer *The Logic of the Humanities.* New Haven, CT: Yale University Press, vii–xviii.

Illeris, K. (2002) *The Three Dimensions of Learning: Contemporary Learning Theory in the Tension Field between the Cognitive, the Emotional and the Social.* Copenhagen, Denmark: Samfundslitteratur.

Irgens, E. J. and Ertsås, T. I. (2008) *Higher Education as Competence Program Providers in a Nationwide School Reform.* In: Nygaard, C., and Holtham, C.: Understanding Learning-Centered Higher Education. Copenhagen: CBS Press, 265–282.

Irgens, E. J. and Hernes, T. (2008) Liminality: On the threshold between learning and non-learning. Article presented at the Organizational Learning, Knowledge and Capabilities Conference, Copenhagen, Denmark, 28–31 April 2008.

Kagan, J. (2010) *The Three Cultures: Natural Sciences, Social Sciences, and the Humanities in the 21st Century.* Cambridge: Cambridge University Press [Kindle version]. Retrieved from Amazon.com.

Kamoche, K. and Cunha, M. P. E. (2001) Minimal structures: From jazz improvisation to product innovation. *Organization Studies,* 22, 733–764.

Knights, D. and Mueller, F. (2004) Strategy as a 'project': Overcoming dualisms in the strategy debate. *European Management Review,* 1(1), 55–61.

Krois, J. M. (2009) *The Priority of "Symbolism" Over Language in Cassirer's Philosophy.* Online 14 July 2009. <http://www.springerlink.com/content/fm8q62663m6ux268/> (accessed 5 July 2010).

Lawrence, P. and Lorsch, J. (1967) Differentiation and integration in complex organizations. *Administrative Science Quarterly,* 12, 1–30.

LeDoux, J. (1996) *The Emotional Brain: The Mysterious Underpinnings of Emotional Life.* New York: Simon & Schuster.

Levinson, W.; Roter, D. L.; Mullooly, J. P.; Dull, V. T.; Frankel, R. M. (1997) Physician-patient communication: The relationship with malpractice claims among primary care physicians and surgeons. *Journal of the American Medical Association,* 277(7), 553–559.

Levinthal, D. A. (1991) Organizational adaptation and environmental selection-interrelated processes of change. *Organization Science,* 2, 140–145.

Levinthal, D. A. and March, J. G. (1993) The myopia of learning. *Strategic Management Journal,* 14, 95–112.

Lewin, K. (1947) Frontiers in group dynamics: Concept, method and reality in social science; social equilibria and social change. *Human Relations,* 1; 5, 5–41.

Linstead, S. and Höpfl, H., eds. (2000) *The Aesthetics of Organization.* London: Sage.

Littlejohn, S. W. (1992) *Theories of Human Communication.* Belmont, CA: Wadsworth Publishing.

Lofts, S. G. (2000) *Ernst Cassirer: A "Repetition" of Modernity.* New York: State University of New York Press.

Maia, T. V. and McClelland, J. L. (2004) From the cover. A reexamination of the evidence for the somatic marker hypothesis: What participants really know in the Iowa gambling task. *Proceedings of the National Academy of Sciences USA,* 101, 16075–16080.

Maia, T. V. and McClelland, J. L. (2005) The somatic marker hypothesis: Still many questions but no answers. Response to Bechara et al. *Trends in Cognitive Sciences,* 9, 162–164.

March, J. G. (1976) "The technology of foolishness," in J. G. March and J. P. Olsen (Eds.) *Ambiguity and Choice in Organizations.* Oslo, Norway: Universitetsforlaget, 69–81.

March, J. G. and Simon, H. A. (1958) *Organizations.* New York: John Wiley & Sons Inc.

Margolis, J. (1986) *Pragmatism Without Foundations: Reconciling Realism and Relativism.* Oxford, England: Blackwell.

Martin, J. (2003) "Meta-theoretical controversies in studying organizational culture," in H. Tsoukas and C. Knudsen (Eds.) *The Oxford Handbook of Organization Theory.* London: Oxford University Press, 392–419.

Matthews, P. M. and McQuain, J. (2003) *The Bard on the Brain: Understanding the Mind Through the Art of Shakespeare and the Science of Brain Imaging.* New York: Dana Press.

Meyer, T. (2006) *Ernst Cassirer.* Hamburg, Germany: Ellert & Richter Verlag.

Mintzberg, H. (1991) Learning 1, planning 0: Reply to Igor Ansoff. *Strategic Management Journal,* 12, 463–466.

Mintzberg, H. (2004) *Managers Not MBAs: A Hard Look at the Soft Practice of Managing and Management Development.* San Francisco: Berrett-Koehler Publishers.

Mintzberg, H. (2009). *Managing.* San Francisco, CA: Berrett-Kohler.

Montuori, A (2003) The complexity of improvisation and the improvisation of complexity: Social science, art and creativity. *Human Relations,* 56(2), 237–255.

Moorman, C. and Miner, A. S. (1998) Organizational improvisation and organizational memory. *Academy of Management Review,* 23(4), 698–723.

Morgan, G. (1986) *Images of Organization.* Newbury Park, CA: Sage.

Morgan, G. (1988) *Riding the Waves of Change: Developing Managerial Competence for a Turbulent World.* San Francisco: Jossey-Bass.

Morgan, G. (1991) "Paradigms, metaphors, and the puzzle solving in organization theory," in J. Henry (Ed.) *Creative Management.* London: Sage, 81–99.

Neher, A. (2005) How perspective could be a symbolic form. *Journal of Aesthetics & Art Criticism*, 63, 359–373.

Newell, S., Robertson, M., Scarbrough, H. and Swan, J. (2002) *Managing Knowledge Work*. Basingstoke: Palgrave.

Nonaka, I. (1991) The knowledge-creating company. *Harvard Business Review*, November–December, 69, 96–104.

Nussbaum, M. C. (2009) Education for profit, education for freedom. *Liberal Education*, 95(3), 5–13.

Nussbaum, M. C. (2010) *Not For Profit: Why Democracy Needs the Humanities*. Princeton, NJ: Princeton University Press.

Orlikowski, W. J. (1996) Improvising organizational transformation over time: A situated change perspective. *Information Systems Research*, 7, 63–92.

Østerberg, D. (2002) "Cassirer and recent constructivist sociology: An assessment," in G. Foss and E. Kasa (Eds.) *Forms of Knowledge and Sensibility: Ernst Cassirer and the Human Sciences*. Kristiansand, Norway: Høyskoleforlaget, 79–92.

Paetzold, H. (2002–1) "Symbol and culture: Cassirer's concept," in G. Foss and E. Kasa (Eds.) *Forms of Knowledge and Sensibility: Ernst Cassirer and the Human Sciences*. Kristiansand, Norway: Høyskoleforlaget, 33–56.

Paetzold, H. (2002–2) "Culture and Critique: Cassirer and the Frankfurt Scool." in G. Foss and E. Kasa (Eds.): *Forms of Knowledge and Sensibility: Ernst Cassirer and the Human Sciences*. Kristiansand, Norway: Høyskoleforlaget, 57–78.

Perrow, C. B. (1970) *Organizational Analysis: A Sociological View*. Belmont CA: Brooks/Cole.

Pondy, L. R. (1978) "Leadership is a language game," in M. W. McCall and M. M. Lombardo (Eds.) *Leadership: Where Else Can We Go?* Durham, NC: Duke University Press, 87–99.

Pondy, L. R. (1989) "Union of rationality and intuition in management action," in S. Srivastva and Associates (Ed.) *The Executive Mind*. San Francisco: Jossey-Bass, 162–191.

Poole, B. and Hitchcock, P. (1998) Bakhtin and Cassirer: The philosophical origins of Bakhtin's carnival messianism. *South Atlantic Quarterly*, 97, 537–578.

Putnam, L. L. (1983) "The interpretive perspective: An alternative to functionalism," in L. L. Putnam and M. E. Pacanowsky (Eds.) *Communication and Organizations: An Interpretive Approach*. Beverly Hills, CA: Sage, 31–54.

Rosile, G. A. and Boje, D. M. (1996) "Pedagogy for the postmodern management classroom: Greenback Company," in D. M. Boje, R. P. Gephart Jr. and T. J. Thatchenkery (Eds.) *Postmodern Management and Organization Theory*. Thousand Oaks, CA: Sage, 225–250.

Røvik, K. A. (1996) "Deinstitutionalization and the logic of fashion," in B. Czarniawska and G. Sevon (Eds.) *Translating Organizational Change*. New York: Walter de Gruyter, 139–172.

Røvik, K. A. (1998) *Moderne organisasjoner: Trender i organisationstenkningen ved tusenårsskiftet*. Bergen, Norway: Fagbokforlaget.

Rynes, S. L., Bartunek, J. M. and Daft, R. L. (2001) Across the great divide: Knowledge creation and transfer between practitioners and academics. *The Academy of Management Journal*, 44, 340–355.

Schein, E. H. (1999) *The Corporate Culture Survival Guide: Sense and Nonsense about Culture*. San Francisco: Jossey-Bass.

Schein, E. H. (2001) "Organizational culture and leadership," in J. Shafritz and J. S. Ott (Eds.) *Classics of Organization Theory*. Fort Worth, TX: Harcourt College Publishers, 369–376.

Scherer, A. G. (2003) "Modes of explanation in organization theory," in H. Tsoukas and C. Knudsen (Eds.) *The Oxford Handbook of Organizational Theory*. Oxford, England: Oxford University Press, 310–344.

Schön, D. (1983) *The Reflective Practitioner. How professionals think in action.* Aldershot, England: Ashgate.

Schön, D. (1987) *Educating the Reflective Practitioner.* San Francisco: Jossey-Bass.

Schön, D. A. (1991) *The Reflective Turn: Case Studies in and on Educational Practice.* New York: Teachers Press, Columbia University.

Scott, W. R. (1995) *Institutions and Organizations.* Thousand Oaks, CA: Sage.

Searle, J. R. (1995) *The Construction of Social Reality.* London: Penguin.

Searle, J. R. (2002) Why I am not a property dualist. *Journal of Consciousness Studies*, 9, 57–64.

Selznick, P. (1957) *Leadership in Administration: A Sociological Interpretation.* New York: Harper and Row.

Senge, P. M. (1990) *The Fifth Discipline. The art and practice of the learning organization.* London: Random House.

Sennett, R. (2008) *The Craftsman.* London: Penguin.

Shenhav, Y. and Weitz, E. (2000) The roots of uncertainty in organization theory: A historical constructivist analysis. *Organization*, 7, 373–401.

Skidelsky, E. (2008) *Ernst Cassirer. The Last Philosopher of Culture.* Princeton, NJ and Oxford, England: Princeton University Press.

Slingerland, E. G. (2010) *What science offers the humanities: Integrating body and culture.* New York: Cambridge University Press. [Kindle version]. Retrieved from Amazon.com.

Spree, A. (2003) Cassirers Baumgarten. *Monatshefte*, 95, 410–420.

Starr-Glass, D. and Schwartzbaum, A. (2003) A liminal space: Challenges and opportunities in accreditation of prior learning in Judaic studies. *Assessment & Evaluation in Higher Education*, 28, 179.

Strati, A. (1998) Organizational symbolism as a social construction: A perspective from the sociology of knowledge. *Human Relations*, 51(11), 1379–1402.

Swabey, W. C. (1949) "Cassirer and metaphysics," in P. A. Schilpp (Ed.) *The Philosophy of Ernst Cassirer.* New York: Tudor, 123–148.

Swanborn, P. G. (1996) A common base for quality control criteria in quantitative and qualitative research. *Quality and Quantity*, 30, 19–35.

Swidler, A. (1986) Culture in action. Symbols and strategies. *American Sociological Review*, 51, 273–286.

Taylor, F. W. (1911) *The Principles of Scientific Management.* New York: Harper Bros.

Taylor, S. S. and Carboni, I. (2008) "Technique & practices from the arts: Expressive verbs, feelings, and action," in D. Barry and H. Hansen (Eds.) *The Sage Handbook of New Approaches in Management and Organization.* Thousand Oaks, CA: Sage, 220–228.

Thomas, P. G. (1996) Beyond the buzzwords: Coping with change in the public sector. *International Review of Administrative Sciences*, 62(1), 5–29.

Thompson, P. (1993) "Postmodernism: Fatal distraction," in J. Hassard and M. Parker (Eds.) *Postmodernism and Organizations.* London: Sage, 183–203.

Tolbert, P. S. and Zucker, L. G. (1996) "The institutionalization of institutional theory," in S. Clegg, C. Hardy and W. R. Nord (Eds.) *Handbook of Organization Studies.* London: Sage, 175–190.

Torbert, W. R.(1989) "Cultivating timely executive action," in Suresh Srivastva and Associates (Ed.) *The Executive Mind.* San Francisco: Jossey Bass, 84–108.

Tsoukas, H. and Chia, R. (2002) On organizational becoming: Rethinking organizational change. *Organization Science*, 13, 567–582.

Turner, V. W. (1979) Frame, flow and reflection: Ritual and drama as public liminality. *Japanese Journal of Religious Studies*, 614, 465–499.

Van Maanen, J. (1995) Style as theory. *Organization Science*, 6, 133–143.

Veiga, J. F., Golden, T. D. and Dechant, K. (2004) Why managers bend company rules. *Academy of Management Executive*, 18, 84–90.

Verene, D. P. (1969) Kant, Hegel, and Cassirer: The origins of the philosophy of symbolic forms. *Journal of History of Ideas*, 30, 33–46.

Vesaas, T. (2002) *The Birds*. London: Peter Owen Modern Classics.

Vince, R. and Saleem, T. (2004) The impact of caution and blame on organizational learning. *Management Learning*, 35, 133.

von Glaserfeld, E. (1995) "A constructivist approach to teaching," in L. P. Steffe and J. Gale (Eds.) *Constructivism in Education*. Hillsdale, NJ: Lawrence Erlbaum, 3–15.

Weick, K. E. (1979) *The Social Psychology of Organizing*. 2nd edition. Reading, MA: Addison-Wesley.

Weick, K. (1982) "Enactment processes in organizations," in B. M. Staw and G. R. og Salancik (Eds.) *New Directions in Organizational Behavior*. Malabar, FL: Robert Krieger Publishing Company, 267–300.

Weick, K. E. (1984) "Managerial thought in the context of action. Patterns of individual and organizational learning," in Suresh Srivastva and Associates (Ed.) *The Executive Mind*. San Francisco: Jossey Bass, 221–242.

Weick, K. E. (1991) The nontraditional quality of organizational learning. *Organization Science*, 2, 116–124.

Weick, K. E. (1993) "Organizational redesign as improvisation," in G. P. Huber and W. H. Glick (Eds.) *Organizational Change and Redesign: Ideas and Insights for Improving Performance*. New York: Oxford University Press, 346–379.

Weick, K. E. (1995). *Sensemaking in Organizations*. Thousand Oaks, CA: Sage.

Weick, K. E. and Gilfillan, D. P. (1971) Fate of arbitrary traditions in a laboratory microculture. *Journal of Personality and Social Psychology*, 17, 179–191.

Wheatley, M. J. (1992) *Leadership and the New Science*. San Francisco: Berrett-Koehler.

Wicks, D. (2001) Institutionalized mindsets of invulnerability: Differentiated institutional fields and the antecedents of organizational crisis. *Organization Studies*, 22, 659.

Wilden, A. (1987) *The Rules Are No Game*. London and New York: Routledge.

Index